THE

REDEEMED CAPTIVE RETURNING TO ZION:

A FA ||||||||||||||||||||| ABLE

D0427767

CAPTIVITY AND DELIVERANCE

OF

MR. JOHN WILLIAMS,

MINISTER OF THE GOSPEL IN DEERFIELD,

WHO IN THE DESOLATION WHICH BEFEL THAT PLANTATION BY
AN INCURSION OF THE FRENCH AND INDIANS, WAS BY THEM
CARRIED AWAY, WITH HIS FAMILY AND HIS NEIGHBOR-
HOOD, INTO CANADA,

DRAWN UP BY HIMSELF.

TO WHICH IS ADDED,

A BIOGRAPHICAL MEMOIR OF THE REVEREND AUTHOR,

WITH

AN APPENDIX AND NOTES,

BY

STEPHEN W. WILLIAMS, A. M., M. D

Published in Cooperation with
THE POCUMTUCK VALLEY MEMORIAL ASSOCIATION

Applewood Books
Bedford, Massachusetts

The Redeemed Captive is reprinted from the 1853 edition published in Northampton by Hopkins, Bridgman and Company.

ISBN 1-55709-118-8

PREFACE

TO THE NEW EDITION.

THE writer of the Memoir of the Rev. John Williams is induced to prepare another edition of " The Redeemed Captive," and lay it before the public, on account of the repeated calls for this work.

A great and growing interest in antiquarian research evinces the eagerness with which the present generation seek after the particular history of their ancestors, and the desire they feel of becoming acquainted with their privations and sufferings, their hardships and dangers, in transmitting to them the beautiful heritage which they now occupy.

This is especially the case with those who now reside in the immediate vicinity of the place where those hardships and privations were endured, and also to their connections, who are scattered over various parts of the country. Many others too will read the thrilling narrative with interest and pleasure.

"The Redeemed Captive " was written and published by the Rev. John Williams, soon after his return from Indian slavery and Jesuitical persecution in 1706 – 7, and has since passed through six editions, the last of which was published in the year 1800 ; consequently the book has been long out of print.

It was my intention to have had an engraved likeness of the Rev. Mr. Williams to accompany this work. His portrait, painted soon after his return from captivity, is now in the hands of some of his descendants, but I have in vain endeavored to procure it for this purpose. I have been more fortunate in obtaining an excellent portrait of his son, the Rev. Dr. Stephen Williams, of Longmeadow, who was taken prisoner with his father, and whose Journal is published in the Appendix to this work. I have also the pleasure of presenting a plate of the old fort-house at Deerfield, where the captives were placed after the sacking of the town, and which has been recently torn down. It was about one hundred and sixty years old when it was demolished. The sills and other timbers were as sound as they were when the house was erected. The old door, filled with nails and gashed with Indian tomahawks, is preserved, and still to be seen at the residence of Henry K. Hoyt, Esq.

Although in my notes I have not pretended to give a genealogical history of the descendants of the Rev. John Williams, yet as the Journal of his son, Stephen, and the extract from a Sermon relating to his daughter, Eunice, were arranged for an Appendix to this work, and inasmuch as the public journals are discussing the claims of Eleazer Williams, grandson of Eunice, as the Dauphin, I have not thought it out of place for me to introduce, at the close of the volume, some testimony bearing upon this question; as some interesting facts respecting the history of Eleazer are personally known by me which may be interesting to the public; and, moreover, as I regard him as my kinsman, and a descendant of the author of "The Redeemed Captive."

STEPHEN W. WILLIAMS.

Deerfield, Massachusetts, 1853.

DEDICATION.

TO HIS EXCELLENCY,

JOSEPH DUDLEY, Esq.,

CAPTAIN GENERAL AND GOVERNOR IN CHIEF, IN AND OVER HER MAJESTY'S
PROVINCE OF THE MASSACHUSETTS BAY, IN NEW ENGLAND, ETC.

SIR, — It was a satirical answer, and deeply re-
proachful to mankind, which the philosopher gave to
that question, What soonest grows old? replied, Thanks.
The reproach of it would not be so sensible, were there
not sensible demonstrations of the truth of it, in those
that wear the character of the ingenious. Such as are
at first surprised at, and seem to have no common rel-
ish of divine goodness, yet too soon lose the impres-
sion : "They sang God's praise, but soon forgat his
works." That it should be thus with respect to our
benefactors on earth, is contrary to the ingenuity of
human nature ; but that our grateful remembrance of
the signal favors of Heaven should soon be worn off

by time, is to the last degree criminal and unpardon-
able.

It would be unaccountable stupidity in me, not to
maintain the most lively and awful sense of divine re-
bukes, which the holy God has seen meet in spotless
sovereignty to dispense to me, my family, and people,
in delivering us into the hands of them that hated us,
who led us into a strange land: " My soul hath these
still in remembrance, and is humbled in me." How-
ever, God has given us plentiful occasion to sing of
mercy, as well as judgment. The wonders of Divine
mercy, which we have seen in the land of our captiv-
ity, and deliverance therefrom, cannot be forgotten
without incurring the guilt of the blackest ingratitude.

To preserve the memory of these, it has been thought
advisable to publish a short account of some of those
signal appearances of divine power and goodness for
us ; hoping it may serve to excite the praise, faith, and
hope of all that love God, and may peculiarly serve to
cherish a grateful spirit, and to render the impressions
of God's mighty works indelible on my heart, and on
those who with me have seen the wonders of the Lord,
and tasted of his salvation. That we may not fall
under that heavy charge made against Israel of old,
Psalm lxxviii. 11, 42. " They forgat his works, and
the wonders he shewed them : They remembered not
his hand, nor the day that he delivered them from the
enemy."

And I cannot, Sir, but think it most agreeable to my duty to God, our supreme redeemer, to mention your Excellency's name with honor, since Heaven has honored you as the prime instrument in returning our captivity. Sure I am, the laws of justice and gratitude (which are the laws of God) do challenge from us the most public acknowledgments of your uncommon sympathy with us, your children, in our bonds, expressed in all endearing methods of parental care and tenderness. All your people are cherished under your wings, happy in your government; and are obliged to bless God for you. And among your people, those who are immediately exposed to the outrages of the enemy, have peculiarly felt refreshment from the benign influences of your wise and tender conduct, and are under the most sensible engagements to acknowledge your Excellency, under God, as the breath of their nostrils.

Your uncommon sagacity and prudence in contriving to loose the bonds of your captivated children; your unwearied vigor and application, in pursuing them, to work our deliverance, can never be enough praised. It is most notorious that nothing was thought too difficult by you to effect this design; in that you readily sent your own son, Mr. William Dudley, to undergo the hazards and hardships of a tedious voyage, that this affair might be transacted with success; which must not be forgotten, as an expression of your great solici-

REDEEMED CAPTIVE RETURNING TO ZION.

THE history I am going to write proves, that days of fasting and prayer, without reformation, will not avail to turn away the anger of God from a professing people; and yet witnesseth how very advantageous gracious supplications are, to prepare particular Christians patiently to suffer the will of God, in very trying public calamities. For some of us, moved with fear, set apart a day of prayer, to ask of God either to spare, and save us from the hands of our enemies, or to prepare us to sanctify and honor him, in what way soever he should come forth towards us. The places of Scripture from whence we were entertained in the forenoon, were Gen. xxxii. 10, 11 : " I am not worthy of the least of all the mercies, and of all the truth, which thou hast showed unto thy servant : — Deliver me, I pray thee, from the hand of my brother, from the hand of Esau, for I fear him, lest he will come and smite me, and the mother with the children." And in the afternoon, Gen. xxxii. 26 : " And he said, Let me go, for the day breaketh. And he said, I will not let thee go, except thou bless me." From which

1

we were called upon to spread the causes of fear, relat-
ing to our own selves, or families, before God ; as
also how it becomes us with an undeniable importunity
to be following God, with earnest prayers for his bless-
ing in every condition.   And it is very observable,
how God ordered our prayers in a peculiar manner, to
be going up to him ; to prepare us, with a right Chris-
tian spirit, to undergo, and endure suffering trials.

Not long after, the holy and righteous God brought
us under great trials, as to our persons and families,
which put us under a necessity of spreading before
him in a wilderness, the distressing dangers and calam-
ities of our relations, yea, that called on us, notwith-
standing seeming present frowns, to resolve, by his
grace, not to be sent away without a blessing.   Jacob
in wrestling has the hollow of his thigh put out of joint,
and it is said to him, " Let me go " : yet he is rather
animated to a heroical Christian resolution to continue
earnest for the blessing, than discouraged from asking.

On Tuesday, the 29th of February, 1703–4, not
long before break of day, the enemy came in like a
flood upon us ; our watch being unfaithful ; — an evil,
the awful effects of which, in the surprisal of our fort,
should bespeak all watchmen to avoid, as they would
not bring the charge of blood upon themselves.   They
came to my house in the beginning of the onset, and
by their violent endeavors to break open doors and
windows, with axes and hatchets, awaked me out of
sleep ; on which I leaped out of bed, and, running to-
wards the door, perceived the enemy making their en-
trance into the house.   I called to awaken two soldiers

The enemy fell to rifling the house, and entered in great numbers into every room. I begged of God to remember mercy in the midst of judgment; that he would so far restrain their wrath, as to prevent their murdering of us; that we might have grace to glorify his name, whether in life or death; and, as I was able, committed our state to God. The enemies who entered the house, were all of them Indians and Macquas, insulted over me awhile, holding up hatchets over my head, threatening to burn all I had; but yet God, beyond expectation, made us in a great measure to be pitied; for though some were so cruel and barbarous as to take and carry to the door two of my children and murder them, as also a negro woman; yet they gave me liberty to put on my clothes, keeping me bound with a cord on one arm, till I put on my clothes to the other; and then changing my cord, they let me dress myself, and then pinioned me again. Gave liberty to my dear wife to dress herself and our remaining children. About sun an hour high, we were all carried out of the house, for a march, and saw many of the houses of my neighbors in flames, perceiving the whole fort, one house excepted, to be taken. Who can tell what sorrows pierced our souls, when we saw ourselves carried away from God's sanctuary, to go into a strange land, exposed to so many trials; the journey being at least three hundred miles we were to travel; the snow up to the knees, and we never inured to such hardships and fatigues; the place we were to be carried to, a Popish country. Upon my parting from the town, they fired my house and barn. We were carried over the river, to the foot of the mountain, about a mile from my house, where we found a great number of our Christian neighbors, men, women, and children, to the number of an hundred, nineteen of which were afterward murdered by the way, and two starved to death, near Cowass, in a time of great scarcity, or famine, the savages underwent there. When we came to the foot of the mountain, they took away our shoes, and gave us in the room of them Indian shoes, to prepare us for our travel. Whilst we were there, the English beat out a company that remained in the town, and pursued them to the river, killing and wounding many of them ; but the body of the army being alarmed, they repulsed those few English that pursued them.

I am not able to give you an account of the number of the enemy slain, but I observed after this fight no great, insulting mirth, as I expected ; and saw many wounded persons, and for several days together they buried of their party, and one of chief note among the Macquas. The Governor of Canada told me, his army had that success with the loss of but eleven men ; three Frenchmen, one of which was the lieutenant of the army, five Macquas, and three Indians. But after my arrival at Quebeck, I spake with an Englishman, who was taken in the last war, and of their religion ; who told me, they lost above forty, and that many were wounded : I replied, " The Governor of Canada said they lost but eleven men." He answered, " 'T is true that there were but eleven killed outright at the taking of the fort, but many others were wounded, among whom was the ensign of the French ; but," said he, " they had a fight in the meadow, and in both en-

gagements they lost more than forty. Some of the
soldiers, both French and Indians, then present, told
me so," said he, adding, that the French always en-
deavor to conceal the number of their slain.

After this, we went up the mountain, and saw the
smoke of the fires in the town, and beheld the awful
desolations of Deerfield. And before we marched any
farther, they killed a sucking child belonging to one of
the English. There were slain by the enemy of the
inhabitants of Deerfield, to the number of thirty-eight,
besides nine of the neighboring towns.* We travelled
not far the first day; God made the heathen so to pity
our children, that though they had several wounded
persons of their own to carry upon their shoulders, for
thirty miles, before they came to the river, yet they
carried our children, incapable of travelling, in their
arms, and upon their shoulders. When we came to
our lodging place, the first night, they dug away the
snow, and made some wigwams, cut down some small
branches of the spruce-tree to lie down on, and gave
the prisoners somewhat to eat; but we had but little
appetite. I was pinioned and bound down that night,
and so I was every night whilst I was with the army.
Some of the enemy who brought drink with them
from the town fell to drinking, and in their drunken
fit they killed my negro man, the only dead person I
either saw at the town, or in the way.

In the night an Englishman made his escape; in
the morning (March 1), I was called for, and ordered
by the general to tell the English, that if any more

---

* See Appendix and Notes.

out of them in our family worship. I was made to
wade over a small river, and so were all the English,
the water above knee deep, the stream very swift; and
after that to travel up a small mountain; my strength
was almost spent, before I came to the top of it. No
sooner had I overcome the difficulty of that ascent, but
I was permitted to sit down, and be unburdened of my
pack. I sat pitying those who were behind, and en-
treated my master to let me go down and help my
wife; but he refused, and would not let me stir from
him. I asked each of the prisoners (as they passed by
me) after her, and heard that, passing through the
above-said river, she fell down, and was plunged over
head and ears in the water; after which she travelled
not far, for at the foot of that mountain, the cruel and
bloodthirsty savage who took her slew her with his
hatchet at one stroke, the tidings of which were very
awful. And yet such was the hard-heartedness of the
adversary, that my tears were reckoned to me as a re-
proach. My loss and the loss of my children was great;
our hearts were so filled with sorrow, that nothing but the
comfortable hopes of her being taken away, in mercy
to herself, from the evils we were to see, feel, and
suffer under, (and joined to the assembly of the spirits
of just men made perfect, to rest in peace, and joy
unspeakable and full of glory, and the good pleasure
of God thus to exercise us,) could have kept us from
sinking under, at that time. That Scripture, Job i. 21,
" Naked came I out of my mother's womb, and naked
shall I return thither: the Lord gave, and the Lord
hath taken away; blessed be the name of the Lord,"—
was brought to my mind, and from it, that an afflicting

God was to be glorified; with some other places of Scripture, to persuade to a patient bearing my afflictions.

We were again called upon to march, with a far heavier burden on my spirits than on my back. I begged of God to overrule, in his providence, that the corpse of one so dear to me, and of one whose spirit he had taken to dwell with him in glory, might meet with a Christian burial, and not be left for meat to the fowls of the air and beasts of the earth ; a mercy that God graciously vouchsafed to grant. For God put it into the hearts of my neighbors, to come out as far as she lay, to take up her corpse, carry it to the town, and decently to bury it soon after. In our march they killed a sucking infant of one of my neighbors ; and before night a girl of about eleven years of age. I was made to mourn, at the consideration of my flock being, so far, a flock of slaughter, many being slain in the town, and so many murdered in so few miles from the town ; and from fears what we must yet expect, from such who delightfully imbrued their hands in the blood of so many of His people. When we came to our lodging place, an Indian captain from the eastward spake to my master about killing me, and taking off my scalp. I lifted up my heart to God, to implore his grace and mercy in such a time of need ; and afterwards I told my master, if he intended to kill me, I desired he would let me know of it ; assuring him that my death, after a promise of quarter, would bring the guilt of blood upon him. He told me he would not kill me. We laid down and slept, for God sustained and kept us.

In the morning (March 2), we were all called be-
fore the chief sachems of the Macquas and Indians,
that a more equal distribution might be made of the
prisoners among them. At my going from the wig-
wam, my best clothing was taken from me. As I
came nigh the place appointed, some of the captives
met me, and told me, they thought the enemies were
going to burn some of us, for they had peeled off the
bark from several trees, and acted very strangely. To
whom I replied, they could act nothing against us, but
as they were permitted of God, and I was persuaded
he would prevent such severities. When we came to
the wigwam appointed, several of the captives were
taken from their former masters, and put into the
hands of others ; but I was sent again to my two
masters who brought me from my house.

In our fourth day's march (Friday, March 3), the
enemy killed another of my neighbors, who, being near
the time of travail, was wearied with her journey.
When we came to the great river, the enemy took
sleighs to draw their wounded, several of our children,
and their packs, and marched a great pace. I travelled
many hours in water up to the ankles. Near night I
was very lame, having before my travel wrenched my
ankle bone and sinews. I thought, and so did others,
that I should not be able to hold out to travel far.
I lifted up my heart to God, my only refuge, to remove
my lameness, and carry me through, with my children
and neighbors, if he judged it best ; however, I desired
God would be with me in my great change, if he
called me by such a death to glorify him ; and that he
would take care of my children, and neighbors, and

bless them; and within a little space of time I was well of my lameness, to the joy of my friends, who saw so great an alteration in my travelling.

On Saturday (March 4), the journey was long and tedious; we travelled with such speed that four women were tired, and then slain by them who led them captive.

On the Sabbath day (March 5), we rested, and I was permitted to pray, and preach to the captives. The place of Scripture spoken from was Lam. i. 18: "The Lord is righteous, for I have rebelled against his commandment: hear, I pray you, all people, and behold my sorrow: my virgins and my young men are gone into captivity." The enemy, who said to us, "Sing us one of Zion's songs," were ready, some of them, to upbraid us, because our singing was not so loud as theirs. When the Macquas and Indians were chief in power, we had this revival in our bondage, to join together in the worship of God, and encourage one another to a patient bearing the indignation of the Lord, till he should plead our cause. When we arrived at New France, we were forbidden praying one with another, or joining together in the service of God.

The next day (Monday, March 6), soon after we marched, we had an alarm; on which many of the English were bound: I was then near the front, and my master not with me, so I was not bound. This alarm was occasioned by some Indians shooting at geese that flew over them, which put them into a considerable consternation and fright. But after they came to understand that they were not pursued by the English, they boasted, that they would not come out after them, as they had boasted before we began our journey in the morning. They killed this day two women, who were so faint they could not travel.

The next day (Tuesday, March 7), in the morning, before we travelled, one Mary Brooks, a pious young woman, came to the wigwam where I was, and told me she desired to bless God, who had inclined the heart of her master to let her come and take her farewell of me. Said she, " By my falls on the ice yesterday, I injured myself, causing a miscarriage this night, so that I am not able to travel far; I know they will kill me to-day; but," says she, " God has (praised be his name !) by his spirit, with his word, strengthened me to my last encounter with death " ; and so mentioned to me some places of Scripture seasonably sent in for her support. " And," says she, " I am not afraid of death ; I can, through the grace of God, cheerfully submit to his will. Pray for me," said she, at parting, " that God would take me to himself." Accordingly, she was killed that day. I mention it, to the end I may stir up all, in their young days, to improve the death of Christ by faith, to a giving them an holy boldness in the day of death.

The next day (Wednesday, March 8), we were made to scatter one from another into smaller companies ; and one of my children was carried away with Indians belonging to the eastern parts. At night my master came to me, with my pistol in his hand, and put it to my breast, and said, " Now I will kill you, for," he said, " you would have killed me with it if you could." But by the grace of God, I was not much daunted, and whatever his intention might be, God prevented my death.

cast out unto the uttermost part of the heaven, yet will
I gather them from thence, and will bring them unto
the place that I have chosen, to set my name there."
These three places of Scripture, one after another, by
the grace of God, strengthened my hopes that God
would so far restrain the wrath of the adversary that
the greatest number of us left alive should be carried
through so tedious a journey; that though my children
had no father to take care of them, that word quieted
me to a patient waiting to see the end the Lord would
make. Jer. xlix. 11, "Leave thy fatherless children,
I will preserve them alive, and let thy widows trust in
me."   Accordingly, God carried them wonderfully
through great difficulties and dangers. My youngest
daughter, aged seven years, was carried all the jour-
ney, and looked after with a great deal of tenderness.
My youngest son, aged four years, was wonderfully
preserved from death; for though they that carried
him or drawed him on sleighs were tired with their
journeys, yet their savage, cruel tempers were so over-
ruled by God that they did not kill him, but in their
pity he was spared, and others would take care of him;
so that four times on the journey he was thus pre-
served, till at last he arrived in Montreal, where a
French gentleman, pitying the child, redeemed it out
of the hands of the heathen. My son Samuel and my
eldest daughter were pitied so as to be drawn on sleighs
when unable to travel; and though they suffered very
much through scarcity of food and tedious journeys,
they were carried through to Montreal: and my son
Stephen, about eleven years of age, wonderfully pre-
served from death in the famine whereof three English

persons died, and after eight months brought into Shamblee.

My master returned on the evening of the Sabbath (March 12), and told me he had killed five moose. The next day (Monday, March 13), we were removed to the place where he killed them. We tarried there three days, till we had roasted and dried the meat. My master made me a pair of snow-shoes; "For," said he, "you cannot possibly travel without, the snow being knee-deep." We parted from thence heavy laden. I travelled, with a burden on my back, with snow-shoes, twenty-five miles the first day of wearing them; and again the next day till afternoon, and then we came to the French river. My master at this place took away my pack, and drew the whole load on the ice; but my bones seemed to be misplaced, and I unable to travel with any speed. My feet were very sore, and each night I wrung blood out of my stockings when I pulled them off. My shins also were very sore, being cut with crusty snow in time of my travelling without snow-shoes. But finding some dry oak-leaves by the river-banks, I put them to my shins, and in once applying them they were healed. And here my master was very kind to me, — would always give me the best he had to eat: and, by the goodness of God, I never wanted a meal's meat during my captivity; though some of my children and neighbors were greatly wounded (as I may say) with the arrows of famine and pinching want, having for many days nothing but roots to live upon, and not much of them neither. My master gave me a piece of a Bible; never disturbed me in reading the Scriptures, or in praying to God.

Many of my neighbors, also, found that mercy in their journey, to have Bibles, psalm-books, catechisms, and good books put into their hands, with liberty to use them; and yet, after their arrival at Canada, all possible endeavors were used to deprive them of them. Some say their Bibles were demanded by the French priests, and never redelivered to them, to their great grief and sorrow.

My march on the French river was very sore, for, fearing a thaw, we travelled a very great pace; my feet were so bruised, and my joints so distorted by my travelling in snow-shoes, that I thought it impossible to hold out. One morning a little before break of day my master came and awaked me out of sleep, saying, "Arise, pray to God, and eat your breakfast, for we must go a great way to-day." After prayer, I arose from my knees, but my feet were so tender, swollen, bruised, and full of pain, that I could scarce stand upon them without holding by the wigwam. And when the Indians said, "You must run to-day," I answered I could not run. My master pointed out his hatchet; said to me, "Then I must dash out your brains and take off your scalp." I said, "I suppose, then, you will do so, for I am not able to travel with speed." He sent me away alone, on the ice. About sun half an hour high he overtook me, for I had gone very slowly, not thinking it possible to travel five miles. When he came up, he called me to run; I told him I could go no faster. He passed by without saying one word more: so that sometimes I scarce saw any thing of him for an hour together. I travelled from about break of day till dark, never so much as sat down at noon to eat warm victuals,— eating frozen meat, which I had in my coat-pocket, as I travelled. We went that day two of their days' journey as they came down. I judge we went forty or forty-five miles that day. God wonderfully supported me, and so far renewed my strength, that in the afternoon I was stronger to travel than in the forenoon. My strength was restored and renewed to admiration. We should never distrust the care and compassion of God, who can give strength to them who have no might, and power to them who are ready to faint.

When we entered on the lake, the ice was rough and uneven, which was very grievous to my feet, that could scarce bear to be set down on the smooth ice on the river. I lifted up my cry to God in ejaculatory requests, that he would take notice of my state, and some way or other relieve me. I had not marched above half a mile before there fell a moist snow, about an inch and a half deep, that made it very soft for my feet to pass over the lake to the place where my master's family was. Wonderful favors in the midst of trying afflictions! We went a day's journey from the lake, to a small company of Indians who were hunting. They were, after their manner, kind to me, and gave me the best they had, which was moose-flesh, ground-nuts, and cranberries, but no bread: for three weeks together I ate no bread. After our stay there, and undergoing difficulties in cutting wood, and suffering by lousiness, having lousy old clothes of soldiers put upon me when they stript me of mine, to sell to the French soldiers in the army, we again began a march for Shamblee. We stayed at a branch of the lake, and feasted two or three days on geese we killed there.

After another day's travel, we came to a river where
the ice was thawed. We made a canoe of elm-bark
in one day; and arrived on a Saturday * near noon at
Shamblee, a small village where is a garrison and fort
of French soldiers.

AT SHAMBLEE.

This village is about fifteen miles from Montreal.
The French were very kind to me. A gentleman of
the place took me into his house and to his table, and
lodged me at night on a good feather-bed. The inhab-
itants and officers were very obliging to me the little
time I stayed with them, and promised to write a letter
to the Governor-in-chief to inform him of my passing
down the river. Here I saw a girl taken from our
town, and a young man, who informed me that the
greatest part of the captives were come in, and that two
of my children were at Montreal; that many of the
captives had been in, three weeks before my arrival.
Mercy in the midst of judgment! As we passed along
the river towards Sorel, we went into a house where
was an English woman of our town, who had been
left among the French in order to her conveyance to
the Indian fort. The French were very kind to her
and to myself, and gave us the best provision they had;
and she embarked with us to go down to St. Francis
fort. When we came down to the first inhabited
house at Sorel, a French woman came to the river-
side and desired us to go into her house; and when we

---

* Suppose March 25.

and prayed a short prayer, and invited me to sup with
them, and justified the Indians in what they did against
us, rehearsing some things done by Major Walden
above thirty years ago, and how justly God retaliated
them in the last war, and inveighed against us for be-
ginning this war with the Indians, and said we had be-
fore the last winter and in the winter been very barba-
rous and cruel in burning and killing Indians. I told
them that the Indians, in a very perfidious manner, had
committed murders on many of our inhabitants after
the signing articles of peace ; and as to what they
spake of cruelties, they were undoubtedly falsehoods,
for I well knew the English were not approvers of any
inhumanity or barbarity towards enemies.   They said
an Englishman had killed one of St. Casteen's rela-
tions, which occasioned this war ; for, say they, the
nations, in a general council, had concluded not to en-
gage in the war on any side till they themselves were
first molested, and then all of them as one would en-
gage against them that began a war with them ; and
that upon the killing of Casteen's kinsman a post was
despatched to Canada to advertise the Macquas and
Indians that the English had begun a war ; on which
they gathered up their forces, and that the French
joined with them to come down on the Eastern parts ;
and that when they came near New England, several
of the Eastern Indians told them of the peace made
with the English, and the satisfaction given them from
the English for that murder ; but the Macquas told
them it was now too late, for they were sent for and
were now come, and would fall on them if without their
consent they made a peace with the English.   Said

ship." To which I answered, that I was not to do evil
that good might come of it, and that forcing in matters
of religion was hateful. They answered, " The In-
dians are resolved to have it so, and they could not
pacify them without my coming; and they would en-
gage they should offer no force or violence to cause
any compliance with their ceremonies." The next
mass, my master bid me go to church. I objected; he
rose and forcibly pulled me by my head and shoulders
out of the wigwam to the church, which was nigh the
door. So I went in and sat down behind the door: and
there saw a great confusion, instead of any Gospel
order; for one of the Jesuits was at the altar saying
mass in a tongue unknown to the savages, and the
other, between the altar and the door, saying and sing-
ing prayers among the Indians at the same time; and
many others were at the same time saying over their
Pater-nosters and Ave Mary by tale from their chapelit,
or beads on a string. At our going out we smiled at
their devotion so managed, which was offensive to
them, for they said we made a derision of their wor-
ship. When I was here a certain savagess died. One
of the Jesuits told me she was a very holy woman, who
had not committed one sin in twelve years. After a
day or two the Jesuits asked me what I thought of their
way now I saw it. I told them I thought Christ said of
it, as Mark vii. 7, 8, 9, " Howbeit, in vain do they wor-
ship me, teaching for doctrines the commandments of
men. For laying aside the commandment of God, ye
hold the tradition of men, as the washing of pots and
cups; and many other such like things ye do. And
he said unto them, Full well ye reject the command-

ment of God, that ye may keep your own tradition."
They told me they were not the commandments of
men, but apostolical traditions, of equal authority with
the Holy Scriptures; and that after my death I would
bewail my not praying to the Virgin Mary, and that I
should find the want of her intercession for me with her
Son; judging me to hell for asserting the Scriptures to
be a perfect rule of faith; and said I abounded in my
own sense, entertaining explications contrary to the
sense of the Pope, regularly sitting with a General
Council, explaining Scripture and making articles of
faith. I told them it was my comfort that Christ was
to be my judge, and not they, at the great day; and
as for their censuring and judging me, I was not moved
with it.

One day a certain savagess taken prisoner in Phil-
ip's war, who had lived at Mr. Bulkley's at Weathers-
field, called Ruth, who could speak English very well
and who had been often at my house, being now pros-
elyted to the Romish faith, came into the wigwam, and
with her an English maid who was taken in the last
war. She was dressed in Indian apparel, and was un-
able to speak one word of English. She could neither
tell her own name nor the name of the place from
whence she was taken. These two talked in the In-
dian dialect with my master a long time; after which
my master bade me cross myself; I told him I would
not; he commanded me several times, and I as often
refused. Ruth said, "Mr. Williams, you know the
Scripture, and therefore act against your own light;
for you know the Scripture saith, 'Servants, obey
your masters'; he is your master and you his ser-

vant." I told her she was ignorant and knew not the meaning of the Scripture; telling her I was not to disobey the great God to obey my master, and that I was ready to die and suffer for God if called thereto. On which she talked with my master: I suppose she interpreted what I said. My master took hold of my hand to force me to cross myself, but I struggled with him, and would not suffer him to guide my hand. Upon this he pulled off a crucifix from off his own neck, and bade me kiss it; but I refused once and again. He told me he would dash out my brains with his hatchet if I refused. I told him I should sooner choose death than to sin against God. Then he ran and took up his hatchet and acted as though he would have dashed out my brains. Seeing I was not moved, he threw down his hatchet, saying he would bite off all my nails if I still refused. I gave him my hand and told him I was ready to suffer: he set his teeth in my thumb-nail and gave a gripe, and then said, "No good minister, no love God, as bad as the Devil," and so left off. I have reason to bless God, who strengthened me to withstand. By this he was so discouraged, as never more to meddle with me about my religion. I asked leave of the Jesuits to pray with those English of our town that were with me; but they absolutely refused to give us any permission to pray one with another, and did what they could to prevent our having any discourse together.

After a few days the Governor De Vaudrel, Governor-in-chief, sent down two men with letters to the Jesuits, desiring them to order my being sent up to him to Montreal, upon which one of the Jesuits went with my two masters, and took me along with them, as also two more from Deerfield, a man and his daughter about seven years of age. When we came to the lake, the wind was tempestuous and contrary to us, so that they were afraid to go over; they landed and kindled a fire, and said they would wait awhile to see whether the wind would fall or change. I went aside from the company among the trees, and spread our case, with the temptations of it, before God, and pleaded that he would order the season so that we might not go back again, but be furthered on our voyage, that I might have opportunity to see my children and neighbors, and converse with them, and know their state. When I returned, the wind was more boisterous, and then a second time, and the wind was more fierce. I reflected upon myself for my unquietness, and the want of a resigned will to the will of God; and a third time went and bewailed before God my anxious cares, and the tumultuous working of my own heart, begged a will fully resigned to the will of God, and thought that by his grace I was brought to say amen to whatever God should determine. Upon my return to the company the wind was yet high; the Jesuit and my master said, " Come, we will go back again to the fort; for there is no likelihood of proceeding in our voyage, for very frequently such a wind continues three days, sometimes six, after it continued so many hours." I said to them, " The will of the Lord be done "; and the canoe was put again into the river, and we embarked. No sooner had my master put me into the canoe, and put off from the shore, but the wind fell, and coming into the middle of the river, they said, " We may go

part with their hearts as my child. At my return to the city, I with a heavy heart carried the Jesuit's letter to the Governor, who, when he read it, was very angry, and endeavored to comfort me, assuring me I should see her, and speak with her ; and he would do his utmost endeavor for her ransom. Accordingly he sent to the Jesuits who were in the city, and bid them improve their interest for the obtaining the child. After some days, he went with me in his own person to the fort. When we came thither, he discoursed with the Jesuits. After which my child was brought into the chamber where I was. I was told I might speak with her, but should not be permitted to speak to any other English person there. My child was about seven years old ; I discoursed with her near an hour ; she could read very well, and had not forgotten her Catechism ; and was very desirous to be redeemed out of the hands of the Macquas, and bemoaned her state among them, telling me how they profaned God's Sabbath, and said, she thought that, a few days before, they had been mocking the Devil, and that one of the Jesuits stood and looked on them. I told her, she must pray to God for his grace every day ; she said, she did as she was able, and God helped her. " But," says she, " they force me to say some prayers in Latin, but I don't understand one word of them ; I hope it won't do me any harm." I told her she must be careful she did not forget her Catechism and the Scriptures she had learnt by heart. She told the captives after I was gone, as some of them have since informed me, almost every thing I spake to her ; and said she was much afraid she should forget her Catechism, having none to instruct her. I saw her once a few days after in the city, but had not many minutes of time with her; what time I had I improved to give her the best advice I could. The Governor labored much for her redemption : at last he had the promise of it, in case he would procure for them an Indian girl in her stead. Accordingly he sent up the river some hundred of leagues for one, and when offered by the Governor it was refused. He offered then an hundred pieces of eight for her redemption, but it was refused. His lady went over to have begged her from them, but all in vain ; she is there still ; and has forgotten to speak English. O that all who peruse this history would join in their fervent requests to God, with whom all things are possible, that this poor child, and so many others of our children who have been cast upon God from the womb, and are now outcasts ready to perish, might be gathered from their dispersions, and receive sanctifying grace from God!

When I had discoursed with the child, and was coming out of the fort, one of the Jesuits went out of the chamber with me, and some soldiers to convey me to the canoe. I saw some of my poor neighbors, who stood with longing expectations to see me, and speak with me, and had leave from their savage masters so to do. I was by the Jesuit himself thrust along by force, and permitted only to tell them some of their relations they asked after were well in the city, and that with a very audible voice ; being not permitted to come near to them.

After my return to the city, I was very melancholy, for I could not be permitted so much as to pray with

the English who dwelt in the same house; and the
English who came to see me were most of them put
back by the guard at the door, and not suffered to come
and speak with me. Sometimes the guard was so
strict, that I could scarce go aside on necessary occa-
sions without a repulse; and whenever I went out into
the city (a favor the Governor himself never refused
when I asked it of him) there were spies to watch me
and to observe whether I spake to the English. Upon
which I told some of the English they must be careful
to call to mind and improve former instructions, and
endeavor to stand at a further distance for a while,
hoping that after a short time I should have more lib-
erty of conversing with them. But some spies sent
out found on a Sabbath day more than three of us in
company together, the number we, by their order pub-
lished, were not to exceed, who informed the priest.
The next day one of the priests told me I had a great-
er number of the English with me, and that I had
spoken something reflecting on their religion. I spake
to the Governor that no forcible means might be used
with any of the captives respecting their religion. He
told me he allowed no such thing. I am persuaded
that the Governor, if he might act for himself, would
not have suffered such things to be done as have been
done, and that he never did know of several things
acted against the English.

At my first coming to Montreal, the Governor told
me I should be sent home as soon as Captain Battis
was returned, and not before; and that I was taken in
order to his redemption. The Governor sought by all
means to divert me from my melancholy sorrows, and

always showed a willingness for my seeing my chil-
dren. One day I told him of my design of walking
into the city : he pleasantly answered, " Go with all
my heart." His eldest son went with me as far as the
door, and saw the guard stop me. He went and in-
formed his father, who came to the door and asked
why they affronted the gentleman going out. They said
it was their order. But with an angry countenance
he said his orders were that I should not be stopped.
But within a little time I had orders to go down to
Quebeck. Another thing showed that many things are
done without the Governor's consent, though his name
be used to justify them ; viz., I asked the priest, after
I had been at Montreal two days, leave to go and see
my youngest child. He said, " Whenever you would
see her, tell me, and I will bring her to you ; for," says
he, " the Governor is not willing you should go thith-
er." And yet, not many days after, when we were
at dinner, the Governor's lady (seeing me sad) spake
to an officer at table who could speak Latin to tell me
that after dinner I should go along with them and see
my two children. And accordingly after dinner I was
carried to see them ; and when I came to the house, I
found three or four English captives who lived there,
and I had leave to discourse with them. And not long
after, the Governor's lady asked me to go along with
her to the hospital to see one of my neighbors who
was sick there.

One day one of the Jesuits came to the Governor
and told the company there that he never saw such
persons as were taken from Deerfield. Said he, " The
Macquas will not suffer any of their prisoners to abide

in their wigwams whilst they themselves are at mass, but carry them with them to the church, and they cannot be prevailed with to fall down on their knees to pray there; but no sooner are they returned to their wigwams, but they fall down on their knees to prayer." He said they could do nothing with the grown persons there, and they hindered the children's complying. Whereupon the Jesuits counselled the Macquas to sell all the grown persons from the fort; a stratagem to seduce poor children. O Lord, turn the counsels of these Ahithophels into foolishness, and make the counsels of the heathens of none effect!

Here I observed they were wonderfully lifted up with pride after the return of Captain Montinug from Northampton with news of success. They boasted of their success against New England. And they sent out an army, as they said, of seven hundred men, if I mistake not, two hundred of which were French, in company of which army went several Jesuits, and said they would lay desolate all the places on the Connecticut River. The Superior of the priests told me their general was a very prudent and brave commander, of undaunted courage, and he doubted not but they should have great success. This army went away in such a boasting, triumphing manner, that I had great hopes God would discover and disappoint their designs. Our prayers were not wanting for the blasting of such a bloody design. The Superior of the priests said to me, "Do not flatter yourselves in hopes of a short captivity; for," said he, "there are two young princes contending for the kingdom of Spain"; and for a third, that care was to be taken of his establishment on the English throne : and boasted what they would do in Europe ; and that we must expect, not only in Europe, but in New England, the establishment of Popery. I said, " Glory not ; God can make great changes in a little time, and revive his own interest, and yet save his poor, afflicted people." Said he, " The time for miracles is past ; and in the time of the last war the King of France was as it were against all the world, and yet did very great things ; but now the kingdom of Spain is for him, and the Duke of Bavaria, and the Duke of Savoy," &c. ; and spake in a lofty manner of great things to be done by them, and having the world, as I may say, in subjection to them.

I was sent down to Quebeck in company of Governor De Ramsey, Governor of Montreal, and the Superior of the Jesuits, and ordered to live with one of the Council ; from whom I received many favors, for seven weeks. He told me it was the priests' doings to send me down before the Governor came down ; and that if I went much to see the English, or they came much to visit me, I should yet certainly be sent away, where I should have no conversation with the English.

AT QUEBECK.

After coming down to Quebeck, I was invited to dine with the Jesuits : and to my face they were civil enough. But after a few days a young gentleman came to my chamber and told me that one of the Jesuits (after we had done dinner) made a few districks of verses, and gave them to his scholars to translate into

3

French. He showed them to me. The import of them was, that the King of France's grandson had sent out his huntsmen, and that they had taken a wolf, who was shut up, and now he hopes the sheep would be in safety. I knew at the reading of them what they aimed at, but held my peace, as though I had been ignorant of the Jesuits' intention. Observing this reproaching spirit, I said in my heart, "If God will bless, let men curse if they please "; and I looked to God in Christ, the great Shepherd, to keep his scattered sheep among so many Romish ravenous wolves, and to remember the reproaches wherewith his holy name, ordinances, and servants were daily reproached. And upon an observation of the time of these verses being composed, I find that near the same time the Bishop of Canada with twenty ecclesiastics were taken by the English as they were coming from France, and carried into England as prisoners of war.

One Sabbath-day morning I observed many signs of approaching rain, — a great moisture on the stones of the hearth and chimney-jams. I was that day invited to dine with the Jesuits; and when I went up to dinner it began to rain a small, drizzling rain. The Superior told me they had been praying for rain that morning, "and lo," says he, "it begins to rain!" I told him I could tell him of many instances of God's hearing our prayers for rain. However, in the afternoon there was a general procession of all orders, — priests, Jesuits, and friars, — and the citizens in great pomp, carrying (as they said), as an holy relic, one of the bones of St. Paul. The next day I was invited to the priests' Seminary to dinner. "O," said they, "we went in procession yesterday for rain, and see what a plentiful rain followed!" I answered, " We had been answered when praying for rain when no such signs of rain or the beginnings of rain had preceded, as now with them, before they appointed or began their procession," &c. However, they upbraided me that God did not approve of our religion, in that he disregarded our prayers and accepted theirs. " For," said they, " we heard you had days of fasting and prayer before the fleet came to Quebeck. God would not regard your prayers, but heard ours, and, almost in a miraculous way, preserved us when assaulted, and refused to hear your fast-day prayers for your preservation, but heard ours for your desolation and our success." They boasted also of their king and his greatness, and spake of him as though there could be no settlement in the world but as he pleased ; reviling us as in a low and languishing case, having no king, but being under the government of a queen ; and spake as though the Duke of Bavaria would in a short time be Emperor. From this day forward God gave them to hear sorrowful tidings from Europe ; that a war had been commenced against the Duke of Savoy, and so their enemies increased ; that their bishop was taken, and two millions of wealth with him. News every year more distressing and impoverishing to them ; and the Duke of Bavaria so far from being Emperor that he was dispossessed of his dukedom ; and France so far from being strengthened by Spain, that the kingdom of Spain was like to be an occasion of weakening and impoverishing their own kingdom ; they themselves so reporting. And their great army going against New England turned back ashamed ;

and they discouraged and disheartened, and every year very exercising fears and cares as to the savages who lived up the river. Before the return of that army, they told me we were led up and down and sold by the heathens as sheep for the slaughter, and they could not devise what they should do with us, we should be so many prisoners when the army returned. The Jesuits told me it was a great mercy that so many of our children were brought to them, and that now, especially since they were not like speedily to be returned, there was hope of their being brought over to the Romish faith. They would take the English children born among them, and, against the consent of their parents, baptize them. One Jesuit came to me and asked whether all the English at Loret (a place not far from Quebeck, where the savages lived) were baptized. I told him they were. He said, "If they be not, let me know of it, that I may baptize them, for fear they should die, and be damned if they die without baptism." Says he, "When the savages went against you, I charged them to baptize all children before they killed them; such was my desire of your eternal salvation, though you were our enemies." There was a gentleman, called Monsieur de Beauville, a captain, the brother of the Lord Intendant, who was a good friend to me and very courteous to all the captives; he lent me an English Bible, and when he went to France gave it to me.

All means were used to seduce poor souls. I was invited one day to dine with one of chief note. As I was going, I met with the Superior of the Jesuits coming out of the house, and he came in after dinner; and presently it was propounded to me, if I would stay among them and be of their religion I should have a great and honorable pension from the king every year. The Superior of the Jesuits turned to me and said: "Sir, you have manifested much grief and sorrow for your separation from so many of your neighbors and children: if you will now comply with this offer and proposal, you may have all your children with you; and here will be enough for an honorable maintenance for you and them." I answered: "Sir, if I thought your religion to be true, I would embrace it freely without any such offer; but so long as I believe it to be what it is, the offer of the whole world is of no more value to me than a blackberry"; and manifested such an abhorrence of this proposal, that I speedily went to take my leave and begone. "O, Sir," said he, "sit down; — why in such a hurry? You are alone in your chamber; divert yourself a little longer"; and fell to other discourse. And within half an hour says again: "Sir, I have one thing earnestly to request of you; I pray you pleasure me." I said, "Let your Lordship speak." Said he, "I pray come to the palace to-morrow morning, and honor me with your company in my coach to the great church, it being then a saint's day." I answered, "Ask me any thing wherein I can serve you with a good conscience, and I am ready to gratify you; but I must ask your excuse here"; and immediately went away from him. Returning to my chamber, I gave God thanks for his upholding me; and also made an inquiry with myself, whether I had by any action given encouragement for such a temptation.

AT CHATEAUVICHE (fifteen miles below Quebeck).

Not many days after, and a few days before Governor De Vaudrel's coming down, I was sent away fifteen miles down the river, that I might not have an opportunity of conversation with the English. I was courteously treated by the French and the priest of that parish. They told me he was one of the most learned men in the country. He was a very ingenious man, zealous in their way, but yet very familiar. I had many disputes with the priests who came thither; and when I used their own authors to confute some of their positions, my books, borrowed of them, were taken away from me, for they said I made an ill use of them; they having many of them boasted of their unity in doctrine and profession, and were loath I should show them, from their own best approved authors, as many different opinions as they could charge against us. Here, again, a gentleman, in the presence of the old bishop and a priest, offered me his house and whole living, with assurance of honor, wealth, and employment, if I would embrace their ways. I told them I had an indignation of soul against such offers, on such terms, as parting with what was more valuable than all the world; alleging, " What is a man profited if he gain the whole world, and lose his own soul ? or what shall a man give in exchange for his soul ? " I was sometimes told I might have all my children if I would comply, and must never expect to have them on any other terms. I told them my children were dearer to me than all the world, but I would not deny Christ and his truths for the having of them with me ; I would still put my trust in God, who could perform all things for me.

I am persuaded that the priest of that parish where I kept, abhorred their sending down the heathen to commit ravages against the English; saying it was more like committing murders than managing a war. In my confinement in this parish, I had my undisturbed opportunities to be humbly imploring grace for ourselves, for soul and body; for his protecting presence with New England, and his disappointing the bloody designs of his enemies; that God would be a little sanctuary to us in a land of captivity; and that our friends in New England might have grace to make a more thankful and faithful improvement of the means of grace than we had done, who by our neglects find ourselves out of God's sanctuary.

On the 21st of October, 1704, I received some letters from New England, with an account that many of our neighbors escaped out of the desolations in the fort, and that my dear wife was decently buried, and that my eldest son, who was absent in our desolation, was sent to college and provided for; which occasioned thanksgiving to God in the midst of afflictions, and caused prayers even in Canada to be going daily up to heaven for a blessing on benefactors shewing such kindness to the desolate and afflicted.

The consideration of such crafty designs to ensnare young ones, and to turn them from the simplicity of the Gospel to Romish superstition, was very exercising. Sometimes they would tell me my children, sometimes my neighbors, were turned to be of their religion. Some made it their work to allure poor souls by flat-

teries and great promises, some threatened, some of-
fered abusive carriage to such as refused to go to
church and be present at mass. Some they industri-
ously contrived to get married among them. A priest
drew up a Compendium of the Romish Catholic Faith,
and pretended to prove it by the Scriptures, telling the
English that all they required was contained in the
Scriptures, which they acknowledged to be the rule of
faith and manners; but it was by Scriptures horribly
perverted and abused. I could never come to the sight
of it (though I often earnestly entreated a copy of it)
until I was on shipboard for our vogage to New Eng-
land; but hearing of it, I endeavored to possess the
English with their danger of being cheated with such
a pretence. I understood they would tell the English
that I was turned, that they might gain them to change
their religion. These their endeavors to seduce to
Popery were very exercising to me; and, in my soli-
tariness, I drew up some sorrowful, mournful consider-
ations, though unused to and unskilled in poetry, yet in
a plain style, for the use of some of the captives, who
would sometimes make their secret visits to me, which,
at the desire of some of them, are here made public.

Some Contemplations of the Poor and Desolate State of the Church at Deerfield.

THE sorrows of my heart enlarged are,
Whilst I my present state with past compare.
I frequently unto God's house did go,
With Christian friends his praises for to show;
But now I solitary sit, both sigh and cry,
Whilst my flock's misery think on do I.

Livingston and Mr. Shelden, with letters from his Ex-
cellency our Governor to the Governor of Canada
about the exchange of prisoners, which gave a revival
to many and raised expectation of a return. These
visits from New England to Canada so often greatly
strengthened many who were ready to faint, and gave
some check to the designs of the Papists to gain prose-
lytes. But God's time of deliverance was not yet
come. As to some particular persons, their tempta-
tions and trials were increased, and some abused be-
cause they refused compliance with their supersti-
tions. A young woman of our town met with a new
trial. One day a Frenchman came into the room
where she was, and showed her his beads, and boast-
ed of them, putting them near to her. She knocked
them out of his hands on the floor; for which she was
beaten and threatened with death, and for some days
imprisoned. I pleaded with God his overruling this
first essay for the deliverance of some, as a pledge of
the rest being delivered in due time. I implored
Captain De Beauville, who had always been very
friendly, to intercede with the Governor for the return
of my eldest daughter, and for his purchasing my son
Stephen from the Indians at St. François fort, and for
liberty to go and see my children and neighbors at
Montreal. Divine Providence appeared to the moder-
ating my afflictions, in that five English persons of our
town were permitted to return with Captain Livingston,
among whom went my eldest daughter. And my son
Stephen was redeemed and sent to live with me. He
was almost quite naked, and very poor. He had suf-
fered much among the Indians. One of the Jesuits

took upon him to come to the wigwam and whip him, on some complaints that the squaws had made, that he did not work enough for them. As to my petition for going up to Montreal to see my children and neighbors, it was denied; as my former desire of coming up to the city, before Captain Livingston's coming, was. God granted me favor as to two of my petitions; but yet brought me by his grace to be willing that he should glorify himself in disposing of me and mine as he pleased, and knew to be most for his glory. And almost always before any remarkable favor I was brought to lie down at the foot of God, and made to be willing that God should govern the world so as might be most for his own honor, and brought to resign all to his holy sovereignty; a frame of spirit, when wrought in me by the grace of God, giving the greatest content and satisfaction, and very often a forerunner of the mercy asked of God, or a plain demonstration that the not obtaining my request was best for me. I had no small refreshing in having one of my children with me for four months. And the English were many of them strengthened with hopes that the treaties betwixt the governments would issue in opening a door of escape for all.

In August, Mr. Dudley and Captain Vetch arrived, and great encouragements were given as to an exchange of all in the spring of the year; and some few again were sent home, amongst whom I obtained leave to send my son Stephen.

AT QUEBECK.

Upon Mr. Dudley's and Captain Vetch's petitioning, I was again permitted to go up to Quebec : but disputing with a mendicant friar, who said he was an Englishman sent from France to endeavor the conversion of the English at Quebec, I was, by the priests' means, ordered again to return to Chateauviche ; and no other reason given but because I discoursed with that priest, and their fear that I should prevent his success among the captives. But God showed his dislike of such a persecuting spirit; for the very next day, which was September 20, O. S., October 1st, N. S., the Seminary, a very famous building, was most of it burnt down, occasioned by a joiner's letting a coal of fire drop among the shavings. The chapel in the priests' garden, and the great cross, were burnt, and the library of the priests burnt up. This Seminary and another library had been burnt but about three years before. The day after my being sent away by the priests from Quebec, at first there was a thunder-storm, and the lightning struck the Seminary in the very place where the fire now began.

AT CHATEAUVICHE.

A little before Mr. Dudley's arrival, came a soldier into my landlord's house, barefoot and barelegged, going on a pilgrimage to Saint Anne. "For," said he, " my captain, who died some years ago, appeared to me and told me he was in purgatory, and said I must go a pilgrimage to Saint Anne, doing penance, and get a

mass said for him, and then he should be delivered."
And many believed it, and were much affected with it;
and came and told me of it, to gain my credit of their
devised purgatory. The soldier told me the priests had
counselled him to undertake this pilgrimage, and I am
apt to think ordered his calling in at my landlord's, that
I might see and speak with him. I laughed at the
conceit that a soldier must be pitched upon to be sent
on this errand; but they were much displeased, and
lamented my obstinacy in that I would not be re-
claimed from a denial of purgatory by such a mirac-
ulous providence.

As I was able, I spread the cause before God, be-
seeching him to disappoint them in their expectations
to proselyte any of the captives by this stratagem:
and, by the goodness of God, it was not very service-
able; for the soldier's conversation was such, that sev-
eral among the French themselves judged it to be a
forgery; and though the captain spoken of was the
Governor's lady's brother, I never more heard any con-
cernment or care to get him out of purgatory.

One of the parish where I lived told me, that on the
22d of July, 1705, he was at Quebeck, at the mendi-
cant friars' church, on one of their feast-days, in honor
of a great saint of their order, and that at five o'clock
mass in the morning, near two hundred persons being
present, a great gray cat broke or pushed against some
glass, entered into the church, and passed along near
the altar, and put out five or six candles that were burn-
ing; and that no one could tell which way the cat went
out. And he thought it was the Devil.

AT QUEBECK.

When I was in the city in September, I saw two
English maids who had lived with the Indians a long
time. They told me that an Indian had died at the place
where they were, and that when sundry of his relations
were together in order to attend his funeral, the dead
arose and informed them, that at his death he went to
hell, and there he saw all the Indians that had been dead
since their embracing the Popish religion, and warned
them to leave it off or they would be damned too,
and laid down dead again. They said the Indians
were frightened and very melancholy. But the Jesu-
its, to whom they told this, told them it was only a de-
lusion of the Devil to draw them away from the true
religion; adding, that he knew for certain that all
those Indians who had been dead, spoken of by that
Indian, were in heaven, only one squaw was gone to
hell, who died without baptism. These maids said also,
that many of the Indians much lamented their making
a war against the English, at the instigation of the
French.

AT CHATEAUVICHE.

The priests, after Mr. Dudley's going from Canada,
were ready to think their time was short for gaining
English proselytes, and doubled their vigilance and
wiles to gain over persons to their persuasion. I im-
proved all opportunities I could to write to the English,
that in that way I might be serviceable to them. But
many or most of my letters treating about religion

were intercepted and burnt. I had a letter sent down to me, by order of the Governor, that I had liberty of writing to my children and friends, which should be continued, provided I wrote about indifferent things, and said nothing in them about the points in controversy between them and us; and if I was so hardy as to write letters otherwise, they should endeavor to prevent their being delivered. Accordingly, I found many of them were burnt. Sometimes notice would be given to the English that they were burnt; so that their writing was somewhat useful, though never perused by the English, because they judged those letters condemned Popery. Many of our letters written from New England were never delivered, because of some expressions about religion in them. And, as I said before, after Mr. Dudley's departure from Quebeck, endeavors were very vigorous to seduce. Some were flattered with large promises, others were threatened and beaten because they would not turn. And when two Englishwomen, who had always opposed their religion, were sick in the hospital, they kept with them night and day till they died, and their friends were kept from coming to visit them. After their death, they gave out that they died in the Romish faith, and were received into their communion. Before their death, masses were said for them, and they were buried in the church-yard with all their ceremonies. And after this, letters were sent into all parts to inform the English that these two women turned to their religion before their death, and that it concerned them to follow their example; for they could not be more obstinate than those women were in their health against the

Romish faith, and yet on a death-bed they embraced it. They told the English who lived near, that our religion was a dangerous religion to die in. But I shall hereafter relate the just grounds we have to think these things were falsehoods.

I received a letter from one of my neighbors, wherein he thus bewails : " I obtained leave of my master to go to the Macqua fort to see my children, that I had not seen for a long time. I carried a letter from my master to show that I had leave to come. When I came to the fort, I heard that one of my children was in the woods. I went to see a boy I had there, who lived with one of the Jesuits. I had just asked him of his welfare : he said his master would come presently ; he durst not stay to speak with me now, being in such awe of his master. On which I withdrew ; and when his master came in, I went and asked leave of him to speak with my child, and showed him my letter. But he absolutely refused to let me see or speak with him ; and said I had brought no letter from the Governor, and would not permit me to stay in the fort, though I had travelled on foot near fifty miles for no other errand than to see and speak with my children."

The same person, with another Englishman, last spring obtained leave of the Governor-General to go to the same fort on the same errand, and carried letters from the Governor to the Jesuits, that he might be permitted to speak with his children. The letter was delivered to the Jesuits ; who told him his son was not at home, but gone a hunting ; whereas he was hid from them, as he heard afterwards. So the poor man lost his labor a second time. These men say, that when they returned to Montreal, one Laland, who was appointed as a spy always to observe the motions of the English, told them that one of the Jesuits had come in before them, and had told the Governor that the lad was gone a hunting; and that the Englishman who accompanied this poor man went out into the woods in hopes of finding the lad, and saw him, but the lad run away; and that he followed him and called after him, but he would not stop, but, holding out a gun, threatened to shoot him down if he followed him, and so he was discouraged and turned back; and, says Laland, "You will never leave going to see your children and neighbors till some of you are killed." But the men told him it was an absolute lie, let who would report it; for they had neither seen the lad, nor did they go into the woods to search after him. They judge this was told to the Governor to prevent any English for the future going to see their children and neighbors. Some say they have been promised to have their children who are among the savages, in case they themselves would embrace Popery; and that the priests had said they had rather the children should be among the Indians, as they were, than be brought out by the French, and so be in a readiness to return for New England.

A maid of our town was put into a religious house among the nuns for more than two years, and all sorts of means, by flatteries, threatenings, and abusive carriage, used to bring her to turn. They offered her money, which, when refused, especially the latter part of the time, they threatened her very much; sent for her before them, commanded her to cross herself. They ordered a rod with six branches full of knots to

4

be brought, and, when she refused, they struck her on the hands, still renewing their commands; and she stood to her refusals till her hands were filled with wales from the blows. But one said, " Beat her no more; we will give her to the Indians if she will not turn." They pinched her arms till they were black and blue, and made her go into their church; and because she would not cross herself, struck her several blows with their hands on her face. A squaw was brought in, and said she was sent in to fetch her to the Indians; but she refused. The squaw went away, and said she would bring her husband with her to-morrow, and she should be carried away by force. She told me she remembered what I told her one day, after the nuns had threatened to give her away to the Indians, — that they only said so to affright her; that they would never give her away. The nuns told her she should not be permitted any more to speak to the English, and that they would afflict her, without giving her any rest, if she refused. But God preserved her from falling. This poor girl had many prayers going up to heaven for her daily, and by name, because her trials were more known to the English than the trials of others who lived more remote from them.

Here might be an history by itself of the trials and sufferings of many of our children and young ones, who have been abused, and, after separation from grown persons, made to do as they would have them.

I shall here give an account of what was done to one of my children, a boy between fifteen and sixteen years of age, two hundred miles distant from me, which occasioned a grief and sorrow that I want words to utter; and yet he was kept under such awe, that he never durst write any thing to me, for fear of being discovered in writing about religion. They threatened to put him to the Indians again, if he would not turn; telling him he was never bought out of their hands, but only sojourned with them; but if he would turn, he should never be put into their hands any more. The priests would spend whole days in urging him. He was sent to school to learn to read and write French. The schoolmaster sometimes flattered him with promises if he would cross himself, then threatened him if he would not. But when he saw flattering promises of rewards, and threatenings, were ineffectual, he struck him with a stick he had in his hand; and when he saw that would not do, he made him get down on his knees about an hour, and then came and bid him make the sign of the cross, and that without any delay. He still refused. Then he gave him a couple of strokes with a whip he had in his hand, — which whip had three branches, and about twelve great knots tied to it, — and again bid him make the sign of the cross; and if it was any sin, he would bear it himself; and said also, " You are afraid you shall be changed if you do it; but," said he, " you will be the same; your fingers wont be changed." And after he had made him shed many tears under his abuses and threatenings, he told him he would have it done : and so, through cowardice and fear of the whip, he made the sign, and did so for several days together, and with much ado, he was first brought to cross himself, and then the master told him he would have it done without his particular bidding him. And when he came to say his lesson and

crossed not himself, the master said, " Have you forgot
what I bid you do ? " " No, Sir," said he. Then the
schoolmaster said, " Down on your knees "; and so
kept him for an hour and a half, till school was done ;
and so did for about a week. When he saw this
would not do, he took the whip. " What! wont you
do it ? " said he ; " I will make you "; and so again
frightened him to a compliance. After this, he com-
manded him to go to church. When he refused, he
told him he would make him ; and one morning sent
four of the biggest boys of the school to draw him by
force to mass. These, with other severities and witty
stratagems, were used, and I utterly ignorant of any
attempt made upon him to bring him to change his re-
ligion. Hearing of an opportunity of writing to him
by one of the parish where I was, going up to Mont-
real, I wrote a letter to him, and had by him a letter
from my son, which I shall here insert.

     " HONORED FATHER : —

    " I have received your letter bearing date January
11th, 1705 – 6, for which I give you many thanks, with
my duty, and my brother's. I am sorry you have not
received all the letters I have wrote to you ; as I have
not received all yours. According to your good coun-
sel, I do almost every day read something of the Bible,
and so strengthen my faith. As to the captives newly
brought, Lancaster is the place of two of them, and
Marlborough that of the third ; the Governor of Mont-
real has them all three. There is other news that will
seem more strange to you, — that two Englishwomen,
who in their lifetime were dreadfully set against the

of November, at three o'clock in the afternoon.   The
next day the priests did commend the woman's soul to
the prayers of the congregation in the mass.   In the
afternoon she was honorably buried in the church-yard
next to the church, close to the body of the justice
Pese's wife ; all the people being present at her funer-
al.   The same day, in the evening, Mr. Meriel, with
an Englishwoman, went to Esther Jones.   She did at
first disdain ; but a little while after, she confessed there
were seven sacraments, Christ's body present, the sa-
crament of the Mass, the inequality of power among the
pastors of the Church ; and being returned to wait by
her all night long, he read and expounded to her some
of the Catholic Confession of Faith to her satisfaction.
About midnight he asked whether she might not con-
fess her sins.   ' I doubt not but I may,' said she ; and
two hours after, she made unto him fervent confession
of all the sins of her whole life.   When he said he
was to offer Christ to his Father for her, she liked it
very well.   The Superior of the nuns being come to
see her, she now desired that she might receive Christ's
body before she died.   She did also show Mrs. Stilson
a great mind to receive the sacrament of Extreme Unc-
tion ; and said, that if ever she should recover and get
home, she would reproach the ministers for their neg-
lecting that sacrament, so plainly commanded by St.
James.   In the afternoon, after she had begged pardon
for her wavering, the Catholic Confession of Faith
was read aloud to her, in the hearing of Mr. Craston,
Mrs. Stilson, and another Englishwoman, and she
owned the same.   About seven o'clock the same day,
she said to Mr. Dubison, ' Shall not they give me the

himself, that, if he was in my case, he should be willing
to know the worst, and therefore told me as he would
have desired to have known if in my place. I thanked
him, acknowledging it a favor to let me know of it.
But the news was ready to overwhelm me with grief
and sorrow. I made my complaint to God, and
mourned before him; sorrow and anguish took hold
upon me. I asked of God to direct me what to do, and
how to write, and find out an opportunity of conveying
a letter to him; and committed this difficulty to his
providence. I now found a greater opposition to a pa-
tient, quiet, humble resignation to the will of God, than
I should otherwise have known, if not so tried. Here
I thought of my afflictions and trials, — my wife and
two children killed, and many of my neighbors; and
myself, and so many of my children and friends, in a
Popish captivity, separated from our children, not ca-
pable to come to them to instruct them in the way they
ought to go; and cunning, crafty enemies, using all
their subtilty to insinuate into young ones such princi-
ples as would be pernicious. I thought with myself
how happy many others were in that they had their
children with them, under all advantages to bring them
up in the nurture and admonition of the Lord; whilst
we were separated one from another, and our children
in great peril of embracing damnable doctrines. O
that all parents who read this history would bless God
for the advantage they have of educating their chil-
dren, and faithfully improve it! I mourned when I
thought with myself that I had one child with the Mac-
quas, a second turned to Popery, and a little child, of
six years of age, in danger to be instructed in Popery;

and knew full well that all endeavors would be used to prevent my seeing or speaking with them. But in the midst of all these, God gave me a secret hope that he would magnify his power and free grace, and disappoint all their crafty designs. When I looked on the right hand and on the left, all refuge failed, and none showed any care for my soul. But God brought that word to uphold me, " who is able to do exceeding abundantly above what we can ask or think." As also that, " Is any thing too hard for God ? " I prayed to God to direct me. I therefore replied with the following letter.

"Son Samuel : —

" Yours of January 23d I received, and with it had the tidings that you had made an abjuration of the Protestant faith for the Romish, — news that I heard with the most distressing and sorrowful spirit. O, I pity you, I mourn over you day and night ! O, I pity your weakness, that through the craftiness of man you are turned from the simplicity of the Gospel ! I persuade myself you have done it through ignorance. O, why have you neglected to ask a father's advice in an affair of so great importance as the change of religion ? God knows that the catechism in which I instructed you is according to his word ; and so will be found in the day of judgment. O, consider and bethink yourself what you have done ! And whether you ask me or not, my poor child, I cannot but pray for you, that you may be recovered out of the snare you are taken in. Read the Bible ; pray in secret ; make Christ's righteousness your only plea before God for justification; beware of all immorality, and of profaning God's Sabbaths. Let a father's advice be asked, for the future, in all things of weight and moment. ' What is a man profited, if he gain the whole world, and lose his own soul? Or what shall a man give in exchange for his soul?' I desire to be humbled under the mighty hand of God thus afflicting me. I would not do as you have done for ten thousand worlds. My heart aches within me, but I will yet wait upon the Lord. To him will I commit your case day and night. He can perform all things for me and mine, and can yet again recover you from your fall. He is a ' God, forgiving iniquity, transgression, and sin. To the Lord our God belong forgivenesses, though we have rebelled.' I charge you not to be instrumental to ensnare your poor brother Wareham, or any other, and so add sin to sin. Accept of my love, and don't forsake a father's advice, who above all things desires that your soul may be saved in the day of the Lord."

What I mournfully wrote, I followed with my poor cries to God in heaven to make effectual, to cause in him a consideration of what he had done. God saw what a proud heart I had, and what need I had to be so answered out of the whirlwind, that I might be humbled before him. Not having any answer to my letter for some weeks, I wrote the following letter, as I was enabled of God, and sent to him by a faithful hand; which, by the blessing of God, was made effectual for his good, and the good of others, who had fallen to Popery; and for the establishing and strengthening of

honor due to Christ alone.' The holy Apostle says,
' Now unto him that is able to keep you, and present
you faultless before the presence of his glory, with ex-
ceeding joy, to the only wise God our Saviour, be
glory and majesty, dominion and power, both now and
ever. Amen.' (Jude, ver. 24, 25.) As to what you
write about praying to the Virgin Mary and other
saints, I make this reply: Had Mr. Meriel done his
duty, he would have said to them, as 1 John ii. 1, 2, ' If
any man sin, we have an advocate with the Father,
Jesus Christ the righteous; and he is the propitiation
of our sins.' The Scriptures say, ' There is one God,
and one mediator between God and man, the man
Christ Jesus.' Yea, Christ said, ' Go and preach, He
that believeth and is baptized shall be saved.' The
Apostle, in Gal. i. 8, saith, ' But though we or an angel
from heaven preach any other gospel unto you than
that we have preached to you, let him be accursed.'
They never preached that we should pray to the Virgin
Mary, or other saints. As you would be saved, hear
what the Apostle saith, Heb. iv. 13, &c.: ' Neither is
there any creature that is not manifest in his sight;
but all things are naked and open unto the eyes of him
with whom we have to do. Seeing, then, that we have
a great high-priest, that is entered into heaven, Jesus
the Son of God, let us hold fast our profession. For we
have not an high-priest that cannot be touched with
the feeling of our infirmities, but was in all points
tempted like as we are, yet without sin. Let us there-
fore come boldly unto the throne of grace, that we
may obtain mercy and find grace to help in time of
need.' Which words do hold forth, how that Jesus

them is not humility, but will-worship. Col. ii. 18,
'Let no man beguile you of your reward, in a volun-
tary humility, worshipping of angels'; ver. 23, 'which
things indeed have a show of wisdom and will-worship
and humility.' For what humility can it be to distrust
the way that God has provided and encouraged us to
come to him in, and impose upon God a way of our
own devising? Was not God angry with Jeroboam
for imposing upon him after such a sort? 1 Kings
xii. 33, 'So he offered upon the altar which he had
made in Bethel, the fifth day of the eighth month,
which he devised of his own heart.' Therefore Christ
saith, Mark vii. 7, 'Howbeit, in vain do they worship
me, teaching for doctrines the commandments of men.'
Before the coming of Christ and his entering into
heaven as an intercessor, — Heb. vii. 25, 'Wherefore
he is able to save them to the uttermost that come to
God by him, seeing he ever liveth to make intercession
for them,' — I say, before Christ's entering into heaven
as an intercessor, not one word of any prayer to
saints. What reason can be given that now there is
need of so many saints to make intercession, when
Christ as a priest is entered into heaven to make inter-
cession for us? The answer that the Romanists give
is a very fable and falsehood; viz. that there were no
saints in heaven till after the resurrection and ascen-
sion of Christ, but were reserved in a place called
Limbus Patrum, and so had not the beatifical vision.
See Gen. v. 24: 'Enoch walked with God and was
not, for God took him.' If he was not taken into
heaven, what can be the sense of those words, 'for
God took him'? Again, 2 Kings ii. 1, 'When the

him, and fell down at his feet and worshipped him;
but Peter took him up, saying, Stand up; I myself also
am a man.' See also Lev. xix. 10. The words of the
second commandment, — which the Romanists either
leave out, or add to the first commandment, saying,
'Thou shalt have no other gods before me,' adding,
&c., — I say, the words of the second commandment
are, 'Thou shalt not make to thyself any graven
image, or any likeness of any thing that is in heaven
above, or that is in the earth beneath, or that is in the
waters under the earth; thou shalt not bow down thy-
self to them, nor serve them, for I the Lord thy God
am a jealous God,' &c. These words being inserted
in the letter that came from your brother Eleazer in
New England, the last summer, was the cause of the
letter's being sent down from Montreal, and not given
to you when so near you, as I suppose, there being no
other clause of the letter that could be objected against;
and the reason why found at Quebeck, when I sent it to
you a second time, inclosed in a letter written by my-
self. The brazen serpent made by divine appointment
as a type of Christ, when abused to superstition, was by
reforming Hezekiah broken in pieces. As to what the
Romanists plead about the lawfulness of image and
saint worship from those likenesses of things made in
Solomon's temple, it is nothing to the purpose. We
do not say it is unlawful to make or have a picture, but
those carved images were not in the temple to be
adored, bowed down to, or worshipped. There is no
manner of consequence, that because there were im-
ages made in Solomon's temple that were not made
and worshipped, that therefore it is now lawful to

make and fall down before images, and pray to them,
and so worship them. Religious worshipping of saints
cannot be defended from, but is forbidden in, the Scrip-
tures; and for fear of losing their disciples, the Ro-
manists keep away from them the Bible, and oblige
them to believe as they say they must believe. As
though there was no use to be made of our reason
above our souls; and yet the Bereans were counted
noble, for searching the Scriptures to see whether the
things preached by St. Paul were so or not. They
dare not allow you liberty to speak with your father or
others, for fear their errors should be discovered to
you.

"Again, you write that Esther Jones confessed that
there ' was an inequality of power among the pastors
of the Church.' An argument to convince the world,
that because the priests, in fallacious ways, caused a
woman distempered with a very high fever, if not dis-
tracted, to say she confessed there was an inequality of
power among the pastors of the Church, therefore all
the world are obliged to believe that there is a Pope :
an argument to be sent from Dan to Beersheba, every-
where, where any English captives are, to gain their
belief of a Pope. Can any rational man think that
Christ, in the sixteenth chapter of Matthew, gave St.
Peter such a power as the Papists speak of, or that the
disciples so understood Christ, when immediately there
arose a dispute among them who should be the greatest
in the kingdom of heaven? Matt. xviii. 1, ' At the
same time came the disciples of Jesus, saying, Who is
the greatest in the kingdom of heaven ? ' The Rock
spoken of in the sixteenth of Matthew, not the person

5

of Peter, but the confession made by him; and the
same power is given to all the disciples, if you com-
pare one Scripture with another; not one word in any
place of Scripture of such a vicarship power as of a
Pope, nor any solid foundation of proof that Peter had
a greater authority than the rest of the Apostles. 1 Cor.
iv. 6, 'That you might learn in us not to think of men
above that which is written.' Yea, the Apostle con-
demns them, 1 Cor. i. 12, for their contentions, one
saying, I am of Paul, I of Apollos, and I of Cephas;
no more of Peter's being a foundation than any of the
rest. 'For we are built upon the foundation of the
apostles and prophets, Jesus Christ himself being the
chief corner-stone.' Not one word in any of Peter's
Epistles showing that he had greater power than the
other Apostles. Nay, if the Scriptures give any prefer-
ence, it is to St. Paul rather than St. Peter. 1 Cor. iii.
10, 'According to the grace of God which is given to
me, as a wise master-builder, I have laid the founda-
tion.' 1 Cor. v. 3, 4, 'For I verily, as absent in body,
but present in spirit, have judged already, as though I
were present, concerning him that hath so done this
deed; in the name of our Lord Jesus Christ, when ye
are gathered together, and my spirit, with the power of
our Lord Jesus Christ,' &c. 1 Cor. vii. 1, 'Now con-
cerning the things whereof ye wrote to me'; applica-
tion made, not to St. Peter, but Paul, for the decision
of a controversy or scruple. 1 Cor. xi. 2, 'Now I
praise you, brethren, that you remember me in all
things, and keep the ordinances as I delivered them to
you.' Either those spoken, Acts xv., or in his minis-
try and Epistles. 2 Cor. ii. 10, 'For your sake forgive

which is not done in eating; besides, the priests themselves will not be so put off. The words, 'This is my body,' doth only intend, this doth signify or represent my body; which will appear if you compare scripture with scripture; for after the consecration the Holy Ghost calls it bread, and the fruit of the vine. Exod. xii. 11, 'It is the Lord's Passover'; that is, it represents it. In all the Evangelists you read of killing and eating the passover, a few lines or verses before these words, 'This is my body'; which plainly show, that our Saviour in the same way of figurative expression speaks of the Gospel sacrament. If these words were taken as the Romanists expound them, he must eat his own body himself, whole and entire in his own hands; and after that each of the disciples eat him entire, and yet he sit at the table whole, untouched at the same time; contradictions impossible to be defended by any rational arguments. Yea, his whole body must be now in heaven, and in a thousand other places, and in the mouth of every communicant at the same time, and that both as a broken and unbroken sacrifice, and be subject to putrefaction. Christ is said to be a door, a true vine, a way, a rock. What work shall we make, if we expound these in a literal manner, as the Romanists do, when they say, 'This is my body,' is meant the real body of Christ in the Eucharist? It is said, 1 Cor. x. 4, 'And did all drink of the same spiritual drink, for they drank of that spiritual rock that followed them, and that rock was Christ.' Was Christ literally a rock, think you? Yea, it is absurd to believe that a priest, uttering a few words over a wafer not above an inch square, can make it a God, or the body of Christ entire, as it was offered on the cross. A blasphemy to pretend to a power of making God at their pleasure, and then eat him, and give him to others to be eaten, or shut him up in their altars; that they can utter the same words, and make a God or not make a God, according to their intention; and that the people are obliged to believe that it is God, and so adore it, when they never hear any word of consecration, nor know the priest's intention.

"As to what you write about the Holy Mass, I reply, It is wholly an human invention; not a word of such a sacrifice in the whole Bible; its being a sacrifice propitiatory daily to be offered, is contrary to the Holy Scriptures. Heb. vii. 27, 'Who needeth not daily, as those high-priests, to offer up sacrifice, first for his own sins, and then for the people's; for this he did once when he offered up himself.' And yet the Romanists say there is need that he be offered up as a sacrifice to God every day. Heb. ix. 12, 'By his own blood he entered in once into the holy place, having obtained eternal redemption for us.' 25 – 28, 'Nor yet that he should offer himself often, as the high-priest entereth into the holy place every year with the blood of others; for then must he often have suffered since the foundation of the world: but now once in the end of the world hath he appeared to put away sin by the sacrifice of himself. As it is appointed unto men once to die, but after this the judgment, so Christ was once offered to bear the sins of many.' Heb. x. 10, 'By which will we are sanctified, through the offering of the body of Jesus Christ once for all.' Ver. 12, 'But this man, after he had offered one sacrifice for sins,

for ever sat down on the right hand of God.' Ver. 14,
' For by one offering he hath perfected for ever them
that are sanctified.' By which Scripture you may see
that the mass is not of divine appointment, but an hu-
man invention. Their evasion of a bloody and an un-
bloody sacrifice is a sham. The Holy Scriptures speak
not one word of Christ's being offered as a sacrifice
propitiatory, after such a sort as they call an unbloody
sacrifice. All the ceremonies of the mass are human
inventions, that God never commanded.

"As to what is in the letter about praying for the
women after their death, is very ridiculous: for as
the tree falls, so it lies; as death leaves, judgment
will find. No change after death from an afflicted to
an happy place and state. Purgatory is a fancy for
enriching the clergy and impoverishing the laity. The
notion of it is a fatal snare to many souls, who sin with
hopes of easily getting priestly absolution at death, and
buying off their torments with their money. The soul
at death goes immediately to judgment, and so to
heaven or hell. Mr. Meriel told me, if I found one
error in our religion, it was enough to cause me to dis-
own our whole religion. By his argument you may
see what reason you have to avoid the religion that is
so full of errors.

" Bethink yourself, and consult the Scriptures, if you
can get them (I mean the Bible). Can you think
their religion is right, when they are afraid to let you
have an English Bible; or to speak with your father,
or other of your Christian neighbors, for fear they
would give you such convictions of truth that they can-
not remove? Can that religion be true that cannot

bear an examination from the Scriptures, that are a
perfect rule in matters of faith ; or that must be upheld
by ignorance, especially ignorance of the Holy Scrip-
tures ?

" These things have I written as in my heart I be-
lieve. I long for your recovery, and will not cease to
pray for it. I am now a man of a sorrowful spirit, and
look upon your fall as the most aggravating circum-
stance of my afflictions ; and am persuaded that no
pains will be wanting to prevent me from seeing or
speaking with you ; but I know that God's grace is all-
sufficient : ' He is able to do exceeding abundantly
above what I can ask or think.' Do not give way to
discouragement as to your return to New England.
Read over what I have written, and keep it with you, if
you can ; you have no friend on earth that wisheth
your eternal salvation more heartily than your father.
I long to see and speak with you, but I never forget
you. My love to you, and to your brother and sister,
and to all our fellow-prisoners. Let me hear from you
as often as you can. I hope God will appear for us
before it be long.

" There are a great many other things in the letter
that deserve to be refuted, but I should be too tedious
in remarking them all at once. Yet would not pass
over the passage in the letter, that Esther Jones con-
fessed that there were seven sacraments. To which I
answer, that some of the most learned of the Romish
religion confessed, without the distracting pains of a
violent fever, and left it on record in print, that it can-
not be convincingly made out from the Scripture that
there are seven sacraments ; and that their most incon-

testable proof is from tradition, and by their traditions they might have found seventeen as well as seven; considering that four Popes, successively, spent their lives in purging and correcting old authors. But no men can out of the Holy Scriptures prove any more than two sacraments of divine institution under the New Testament; namely, Baptism and the Lord's Supper. If you make the Scriptures a perfect rule of faith, as you ought to do, you cannot believe as the Romish Church believes. O, see that you sanctify the Lord himself in your heart, and make him your fear and your dread. 'Fear not them that can kill the body, and after that have no more that they can do; but rather fear him that has power to destroy soul and body in hell-fire.' The Lord have mercy upon you, and show you mercy for the worthiness and righteousness' sake of Jesus Christ, our great and glorious redeemer and advocate, who makes intercession for transgressors. My prayers are daily to God for you and your brother and sister, yea, and for all my children and fellow-prisoners.

"I am your afflicted and sorrowful father,

"JOHN WILLIAMS.

" *Chateauviche, March* 22, 1706."

God, who is gloriously free and rich in his grace to vile sinners, was pleased to bless poor and weak means for the recovery of my child so taken, and gave me to see that he did not say to the house of Jacob, "Seek you me in vain." O that every reader would in every difficulty make Him their refuge! He is an hopeful stay. To alleviate my sorrow, I received the following letter in answer to mine.

"*Montreal, May* 12, 1706.

" Honored Father : —

"I received your letter which was sent by ——,
which good letter I thank you for; and for the good
counsel which you gave me : I desire to be thankful for
it, and hope it will be for the benefit of my soul. I
may say, as in the Psalms, 'The sorrows of death com-
passed me, and the pains of hell gat hold on me : I
found trouble and sorrow ; then called I upon the name
of the Lord : O Lord, I beseech thee, deliver my soul !
Gracious is the Lord and righteous, yea, our God is
merciful.' As for what you ask me about my making
an abjuration of the Protestant faith for the Romish, I
durst not write so plain to you as I would, but hope to
see and discourse with you. I am sorry for the sin I
have committed in changing of religion, for which I
am greatly to blame. You may know that Mr. Meriel,
the schoolmaster, and others, were continually at me
about it; at last I gave over to it, for which I am very
sorry. As for that letter you had from me, it was a
letter I transcribed for Mr. Meriel : and for what he
saith about Abigail Turbet and Esther Jones, nobody
heard them but he, as I understand. I desire your
prayers to God for me, to deliver me from my sins.
O, remember me in your prayers ! I am your dutiful
son, ready to take your counsel.

" Samuel Williams."

This priest, Mr. Meriel, has brought many letters to
him, and bid him write them over and send them, and
so he has done for many others. By this, as also by

Mrs. Stilson's saying " she does not think that either of these women did change their religion before their death," and also, " that oftentimes during their sickness, whilst they had the use of their reason, they protested against the Romish religion and faith," it is evident that these women never died Papists, but that it was a wily stratagem of the priests to advance their religion, for letters were sent, immediately after their death, to use this as a persuasive argument to gain others; but God in his providence gave farther convictions of their fallaciousness in this matter.

For the last summer, one Biggilow from Marlborough, a captive at Montreal, was very sick in the hospital, and in the judgment of all with a sickness to death. Then the priests and others gave out that he was turned to be of their religion, and taken into their communion. But, contrary to their expectation, he was brought back from the gates of death, and would comply with none of their rites; saying, that, whilst he had the use of his reason, he never spake any thing in favor of their religion; and that he never disowned the Protestant faith, nor would he now. So that they were silenced and put to shame. There is no reason to think that these two women were any more Papists than he: but they are dead, and cannot speak. One of the witnesses spoken of in the before-mentioned letters, told me she knew of no such thing, and said Mr. Meriel told her that he never heard a more fervent and affectionate prayer than one which Esther Jones made a little before her death. I am verily persuaded, that he calls that prayer to God, so full of affection and fervor, the " confession made by her of the sins of her

carried himself so in his captivity as to edify several
of the English, and recover one fallen to Popery,
taken the last war; though some were enraged against
him on these accounts, yet even the French where he
sojourned, and with whom he conversed, would say
he was a good man, — one that was very prayerful to
God, and studious and painful in reading the Holy
Scriptures; a man of a good understanding, a desir-
able conversation. In the beginning of his last sick-
ness he made me a visit (before he went to the hos-
pital at Quebeck), as he had several times before, to my
great satisfaction, and our mutual consolation and com-
fort in our captivity. He lived not above two miles
from me, at the island of St. Lawrence, about six
weeks or two months. After his death the French
told me Zebediah was gone to hell, and damned; for,
said they, he has appeared since his death to one
Joseph Egerly, an Englishman who was taken in the
last war, in flaming fire, telling him, " He was damned
for refusing to embrace the Romish religion, when
such pains were used to bring him to the true faith;
and for being instrumental to draw him away from the
Romish communion, forsaking the mass; and was
therefore now come to advertise him of his danger " !
I told them I judged it to be a Popish lie; saying, I bless
God our religion needs no lies to uphold, maintain, and
establish it, as theirs did. But they affirmed it to be
true, telling me how God approved of their religion,
and witnessed miraculously against ours. But I still
told them, I was persuaded his soul was in heaven, and
that their reports were only devised fables to seduce
souls. . For several weeks they affirmed it, telling me,

that all who came over the river from the island
affirmed it to be a truth. I begged of God to blast
this hellish design of theirs; so that in the issue it
might be to render their religion more abominable, and
that they might not gain one soul by such a stratagem.
After some weeks had passed in such assertions, there
came one into my landlord's house, affirming it to be a
truth reported of Zebediah; saying, Joseph Egerly
had been over the river and told one of our neighbors
this story. After a few hours I saw that neighbor, and
asked him whether he had seen Egerly lately. He said,
"Yes." "What news told he you?" "None,"
said he. Then I told him what was affirmed as a
truth; he answered, Egerly said nothing like this to
him, and he was persuaded that he would have told
him, if there had been any truth in it. About a week
after, came one John Boult from the island of St.
Lawrence, a lad taken from Newfoundland, a very
serious, sober lad, of about seventeen years of age.
He had often before come over with Zebediah to visit
me. At his coming in he much lamented the loss of
Zebediah; and told me, that for several weeks they
had told him the same story, affirming it to be a truth,
and that Egerly was so awakened by it, as to go again
to mass every day; urging him, since God in such a
miraculous way offered such conviction of the truth of
their religion, and the falsehood and danger of ours, to
come over to their religion, or else his damnation
would be dreadfully aggravated. He said, he could
have no rest for them day and night; but, said he, "I
told them their religion was contrary to the word of
God, and therefore I would not embrace it; and that

I did not believe what they said." And says he to me,
" One day I was sitting in the house, and Egerly came
in, and I spake to him before the whole family (in the
French tongue, for he could not speak much English),
and asked him of this story. He answered, ' It is a
great falsehood,' saying, ' He never appeared to me,
nor have I ever reported any such thing to any body ' ;
and that he had never been at the mass since Zebe-
diah's death. At the hearing of which, they were si-
lenced and put to shame." We blessed God together,
for discovering their wickedness, and disappointing
them in what they aimed at ; and prayed to God to
deliver us and all the captives from delusions, and re-
cover them who had fallen, and so parted. After
which I took my pen and wrote a letter to one Samuel
Hill, an English captive, taken from Wells, who lived
at Quebeck, and his brother Ebenezer Hill, to make a
discovery of this lying plot, to warn them of their dan-
ger, and assure them of the falsehood of this report ;
but the letter fell into the hands of the priests, and was
never delivered. This Egerly came home with us, so
that they gained nothing but shame by their stratagem.
God often disappoints the crafty devices of wicked
men.

In the latter end of summer, they told me they had
news from New England, by one who had been a cap-
tive at Boston, who said that the ministers at Boston
had told the French captives, that the Protestant re-
ligion was the only true religion ; and that as a con-
firmation of it, they would raise a dead person to life
before their eyes, for their conviction ; and that having
persuaded one to feign himself dead, they came and

prayed over him, and then commanded him, in the name of Christ (whose religion they kept pure), to arise ; they called and commanded, but he never arose ; so that instead of raising the dead, they killed the living, which the bereaved relations discovered. I told them, it was an old lie and calumny against Luther and Calvin, new vamped, and that they only change the persons and place ; but they affirmed it to be a truth. I told them I wondered they were so fond of a faith propagated and then maintained by lying words.

We were almost out of hopes of being returned before winter, the season proving so cold the latter end of September, and were praying to God to prepare our hearts with an holy submission to his holy will, to glorify his holy name in a way of passive obedience, in the winter. For my own part, I was informed by several who came from the city, that the Lord Intendant said, if More returned, and brought word that Battis was in prison, he would put me in prison, and lay me in irons. They would not permit me to go into the city, saying I always did harm when I came to the city, and if at any time I was at the city, they would persuade the Governor to send me back again.

In the beginning of last June, the Superior of the priests came to the parish where I was, and told me he saw I wanted my friend, Captain De Beauville, and that I was ragged ; but, says he, " Your obstinacy against our religion discourages us from providing better clothes." I told him, " It was better going in a ragged coat, than with a ragged conscience."

In the beginning of last June, went out an army

of five hundred Macquas and Indians, with an intention to have fallen on some English towns down Connecticut River, but lighting on a Scatacook Indian, who afterwards ran away in the night, they were discouraged, saying he would alarm the whole country. About fifty or eighty returned. Thus God restrained their wrath.

When they were promising themselves another winter, to draw away the English to Popery, news came that an English brigantine was coming, and that the honorable Capt. Samuel Appleton, Esq. was coming ambassador, to fetch off the captives, and Capt. John Bonner with him. I cannot tell you how the clergy and others labored to stop many of the prisoners. To some liberty, to some money, and yearly pensions were offered, if they would stay. Some they urged to tarry at least till the spring of the year; telling them, it was so late in the year, they would be lost by shipwreck if they went now; some younger ones they told, if they went home they would be damned and burnt in hell for ever, to affright them; day and night they were urging them to stay. And I was threatened to be sent aboard, without a permission to come ashore, if I should again discourse with any of the English who were turned to their religion. At Montreal, especially, all crafty endeavors were used to stay the English. They told my child, if he would stay, he should have an honorable pension from the king every year, and that his master, who was an old man, and the richest in Canada, would give him a great deal; telling him, if he returned, he would be poor, for, said they, " your father is poor, has lost all his estate, it was all burnt ";

but he could not be prevailed to stay. And others were also in like manner urged to stay; but God graciously brake the snare, and brought them out. They endeavored, in the Fall of the year, to prevail with my son to go to France, when they saw he would not come to their communion any more. One woman belonging to the Eastern parts, who had by their persuasions married an English captive taken the last war, came away with her husband; which made them say, they were sorry they ever persuaded her to turn to their religion, and then to marry; for instead of advancing their cause by it, they had weakened it; for now they had not only lost her, but another they thought they had made sure of. Another woman belonging to the Eastward, who had been flattered to their religion, to whom a Bible was denied till she promised to embrace their religion, and then had the promise of it for a little time; opening her Bible whilst in the church and present at mass, she read the fourth chapter of Deuteronomy, and received such conviction whilst reading, that before her first communion she fell off from them, and could never be prevailed with any more to be of their religion.

We have reason to bless God, who has wrought deliverance for so many; and yet pray to God for a door of escape, to be opened for the great number yet behind, not much short of an hundred; many of which are children, and of these not a few among the savages, and having forgot the English tongue, will be lost, and turn savages also in a little time, unless something extraordinary prevent.

The vessel that came for us, in its voyage to Cana-

6

da, struck on a bar of sands, and there lay in very
great hazard for four tides ; and yet they saw reason
to bless God for striking there ; for had they got over
that bar, they would at midnight, in a storm of snow,
have run upon a terrible ledge of rocks.

We came away from Quebeck, October 25 ; and by
contrary winds, and a great storm, we were retarded,
and then driven back nigh the city, and had a great
deliverance from shipwreck, the vessel striking twice
on a rock in that storm. But through God's goodness,
we all arrived in safety at Boston, November 21 ; the
number of captives, fifty-seven, two of which were my
children.   I have yet a daughter of ten years of age,
and many neighbors, whose case bespeaks your com-
passion and prayers to God, to gather them, being out-
casts ready to perish.

At our arrival at Boston, we found the kindness of
the Lord in a wonderful manner, in opening the hearts
of many to bless God with us and for us ; wonderfully
to give for our supplies in our needy state.   We are
under obligation to praise God, for disposing the hearts
of so many to so great charity ; and under great bonds
to pray for a blessing on the heads, hearts, and fami-
lies of them, who so literally and plentifully gave for
our relief.   It is certain, that the charity of the whole
country of Canada, though moved with the doctrine of
merit, does not come up to the charity of Boston alone,
where notions of merits are rejected ; but acts of char-
ity performed out of a right Christian spirit, from a
spirit of thankfulness to God, out of obedience to God's
command, and unfeigned love and charity to them that
are of the same family and household of faith.   The

Lord grant that all who devise such liberal things may find the accomplishment of the promises made by God, in their own persons, and theirs after them, from generation to generation.

I shall annex a short account of the troubles beginning to arise in Canada. On May 16 arrived a canoe at Quebeck, that brought letters from Mississippi, written the May preceding; giving an account that the plague was there, and that one hundred and fifty French in a very little time had died of it; and that the savages called the Lezilouways were very turbulent, and had with their arrows wounded a Jesuit in five places, and killed a Frenchman that waited on him. In July news came that the nations up the river were engaged in a war one against the other; and that the French living so among them, and trading with them, were in great danger; that the Michel Macquinas * had made a war with the Mizianmies, and had killed a mendicant friar, and three other Frenchmen, and eleven savages, at a place called the Straits, where they are settling a garrison and place for traffic; the Michel Macquinas have taken sixteen Frenchmen prisoners, and burnt their trading-houses. These tidings made the French very full of perplexing troubles; but the Jesuits are endeavoring to pacify them. But the troubles when we came away were rather increasing than lessening; for the last letters from the French prisoners at Michel Macquina report that the savages

---

* Michilimackinaws.

had sent out two companies, one of an hundred and fifty, the other of an hundred and sixty, against the savages at the Straits; and they feared they would engage as well against the French as the Indians.

BIOGRAPHICAL MEMOIR

OF

THE REV. JOHN WILLIAMS,

AUTHOR OF "THE REDEEMED CAPTIVE."

MEMOIR.

THE lives of eminent men are identified with the history of the section of the country in which they have resided. This is peculiarly the case with the subject of this memoir. Having spent the greater part of his days in the town of Deerfield, on the banks of Connecticut River, at a period when the country was wild and waste, and exposed to all the horrors of savage warfare, and having sustained so great a share of the privations and sufferings of our fathers in planting and establishing the pleasant country in which we now reside, under the banners of peace, of comfort, and security, his biography must be interesting to his friends and the public.

Mr. John Williams was born at Roxbury, Massachusetts, December 16, 1664. He was son of Deacon Samuel Williams, of the same place, and grandson of Mr. Robert Williams, who, according to the best information I can obtain, came from Norwich, England, and settled at Roxbury in the year 1638, eighteen years from the time of the landing of the Pilgrims at Plymouth, and eight years from the settlement of Trimountain, Shawmut, or Boston. It appears that at the time of the first settlement of Boston there was but one English inhabitant in Roxbury. Eight years after this, Mr. Williams arrived and settled there. We have no correct account of the cause of his leaving his native land, but it was probably on account of the religious persecutions of the Puritans, which at that time were carried on with fiery and unrelenting zeal; — so much so, that our ancestors preferred risking their lives and property in a savage wilderness, far distant from their native home, to the more savage persecutions of fanatical bigots. The faithful page of history has informed us of the sufferings of our fathers in establishing themselves in this howling wilderness, and how much they had to contend with from the warfare of the savages, from famine and disease. It is probable that Mr. Williams endured his portion of these trials and hardships. Soon after his arrival at Roxbury, he married, and had four children, and from him have descended all the families of Williamses in this section of the country.

John, the subject of this notice, early devoted his attention to study. Through the munificence of his honored and pious grandfather, on the maternal side, Deacon William Park, he was educated at Harvard College, and graduated there in the year 1683, at the age of nineteen years. He soon after commenced the study of Divinity. I do not know the period of clerical pupilage in those days, but it appears that he became the first minister of Deerfield in the spring of 1686. The peril of such an undertaking in those days, when the country had been laid in ruins but a short time be-

fore by the bold incursions of King Philip of Mount
Hope, one of the most enterprising chieftains, accord-
ing to his means, of ancient or modern times, was such
as to demand a slight view of the ancient history of the
town of his adoption, and of those scenes of blood and
carnage which our ancestors so largely shared and
suffered, to transmit to us these fertile fields, these
beautiful domains. Although he was not an active
participator in the bloody battles of Lathrop and Tur-
ner, yet they occurred in the age in which he lived,
and on the very ground which he afterwards selected
as the place of his abode, although surrounded by the
same dangers and difficulties with which his immediate
ancestors had to contend. It is therefore necessary
that a slight notice of these events should be incorpo-
rated with the history of his life.

In the year 1651, the General Court of the Massa-
chusetts Bay granted two thousand acres of land to the
Indians for an Indian village at Natick, which was then
a part of Dedham; and in compensation to Dedham
therefor, they granted to the proprietors of Dedham
eight thousand acres of any land heretofore unappro-
priated within the jurisdiction, wherever the proprietors
might choose to locate them.

In 1663 messengers were sent to examine the coun-
try. These were John Fairbanks and Lieutenant Daniel
Fisher, who, on their return, gave a most glowing de-
scription of the land on the banks of Deerfield River,
which account may be found in Worthington's History
of Dedham; and the town of Dedham appointed six
persons to repair to Deerfield, which was then called
by the Indians Pocomptuck, and to locate the eight

thousand acres there. Captain John Pynchon, of
Springfield, was employed by the town to purchase
those lands of the Indians. He soon after performed
that duty, and procured four deeds from the Indians,
which were afterwards deposited in Deacon Aldis's
box at Dedham. Dedham gave ninety-four pounds
ten shillings for these deeds; which sum was procured
by an assessment on the common rights in the Ded-
ham proprietary.

In the spring of the year 1671 the first settlement of
Deerfield began, and a few houses were erected on the
main street, on lots drawn by the proprietors, on the
town plat, which was then a forest. The location of
the eight thousand acres, called the Dedham Grant,
under the administration of Governor Bellingham, be-
gan at Pocomptuck River, near Cheapside, and extend-
ed north so as to contain all the meadow lands, the
town plat, Bloody-Brook village, and all the flat lands
within the hills to Hatfield line, and a better tract of the
same quantity of land could not have been selected,
even by men of the present day. Our ancestors well
knew where to find good lands, or they never would
have perilled life and liberty in an uncultivated and
savage wilderness.

The first inhabitants lived on peaceable terms with
the Indians until the year 1675, at which time King
Philip's war commenced. On the 1st of September of
this year the town was attacked by the Indians, several
houses were burnt, and one man, by the name of
James Eggleston, was killed. On the 12th of the same
month, when going to attend public worship on Sun-
day, the inhabitants were attacked, and a man by the

which was then covered with woods, and had just crossed the little stream now called Bloody-Brook, precisely at the spot where the present bridge now crosses that stream, and exactly at the place where the monument is erected in commemoration of the event, without any warning, they were attacked, probably by King Philip himself and seven or eight hundred ferocious Indians, howling for vengeance, brandishing the deadly tomahawk and murderous scalping-knife. The troops had crossed the stream, and were waiting for the teams to come up. More than one account states that many of the soldiers had stacked or laid down their guns, and, in conscious security, were regaling themselves upon the delicious grapes which were found there in great abundance, growing upon the vines which were entwined around the trees at that place. In a moment the guns of the whole body of Indians, who were lying in wait for their victims, poured destruction upon their ranks, accompanied by the terrific yells of the savage war-whoop Captain Lathrop and the greater part of his soldiers fell on the first attack. Those who remained fought with the ferocity of tigers ; — but of what avail were skill and bravery against such a disparity of numbers ? Of nearly one hundred men who entered that field of death on that fatal morning, in the bloom of health, of youth, of manly beauty, only seven or eight remained to tell the melancholy tale. All the rest were inhumanly butchered, and the clods of the valley have rested upon their bosoms for more than one hundred and sixty years. Departed spirits, farewell ! we have often mourned your early exit and dropped the tear of commiseration at your much-lamented fate. These young men have always been considered "the flower of the county of Essex," and descended from the most respectable families there. Mr. Hubbard, the historian, or Cotton Mather, calls this "the saddest day which ever occurred in New England."

Captain Moseley, who was stationed at Deerfield Street, with Lieutenants Pickering and Savage, either hearing the firing at Bloody-Brook, or being apprised of the disaster of Captain Lathrop by the soldiers or teamsters who were so fortunate as to escape from the massacre, ran immediately to their relief, but was too late for the rescue. They found the Indians plundering the dead of such articles of value as remained about them. They attacked the Indians with great fury, and they were as much unprepared for such an assault as Lathrop was for their attack upon him. They charged them to and fro across the swamp, and destroyed them in great numbers. They finally drove them across a great western swamp, and dispersed them in a distant forest. In all this skirmishing and destruction of the enemy, Captain Moseley lost only two men, and had six or eight wounded.

Towards the close of the day, Major Treat, who was on a march from Hadley to Northfield, arrived upon the field of action with about one hundred men, English, and Pequot and Mohegan Indians; and was of service to Captain Moseley and his men in helping him to disperse the enemy. Treat and Moseley retired to the garrison that night, and in the morning returned to bury Lathrop and his slain, when they found a party of Indians plundering the dead.

I copy from General Hoyt's Antiquarian Researches, a work of standard merit, (and one which I hope will soon pass into a new and more beautiful edition,) the following singular instance of resuscitation from apparent death, which occurred at this time. " One Robert Dutch, of Ipswich, who had been prostrated by a ball which contused his head, mauled by hatchets, stripped, and left for dead, recovered his senses, arose from the ground covered with blood, and in a state of nudity walked up to Moseley's men. He was furnished with clothes, carried to the English headquarters, recovered, and lived several years in perfect health."

The Indians lost on that day about ninety-six men, who were, probably, most of them killed in the engagement with Moseley. About forty years after this event, during the ministry of Mr. Williams, our forefathers erected a rude monument to the memory of Captain Lathrop and his men ; but the different occupants of the soil have removed it so many times, that it has been extremely difficult to ascertain the precise spot where he or his men were buried. So much laudable curiosity has been excited, of late, upon the subject, that a meeting of several of the citizens of the ancient town of Deerfield was held in the summer of 1835, for the purpose of making arrangements for commemorating the hundred and sixtieth anniversary of the destruction of Captain Lathrop and his men, for ascertaining, if possible, where their bones lie interred, and to take measures for the erection of a monument to their memories. The committee of investigation, guided by the tradition of some aged people, were so fortunate as to discover the precise spot where Lathrop and about thirty of his men were buried, and their bones were in a tolerable state of preservation, although they disintegrated upon exposure to the air. The grave is just in front of the door-yard of Stephen Whitney, Esq., and about twenty feet northwest of his front door.

A grave, probably containing the bones of the ninety-six Indians who were slain on that day, was likewise found, by accident, about the same time, nearly one hundred rods west of the head of the road leading from Bloody-Brook to Conway, by Mr. Artemas Williams, and a little more than half a mile southwest of the grave of Lathrop; an admirable situation for an Indian grave.

The Hon. Edward Everett was appointed the orator for the occasion, and General Ep. Hoyt of this town was requested to prepare the address at the laying of the corner-stone for the monument. Extensive preparations were made for the commemoration of the event, and on the day of the celebration the high expectations of the public were not disappointed. About six thousand people listened with enchained attention and rapturous delight to the lofty and thrilling tones of oratory proceeding from both the speakers, who did ample justice to the heroism and valor of our ancestors. Other scarcely less animating addresses and sentiments were given at the table, and the festivities of the occasion were highly exhilarating. A collection of above two hundred dollars was shortly made for the monument, and we trust the crying sin of neglect will no longer rest upon their descendants.

> " Sleep, soldiers of merit, sleep, gallants of yore,
>   The hatchet is fallen, the struggle is o'er ;
>   While the fir-tree is green, or the wind rolls a wave,
>   The tear-drop shall brighten the turf of the brave."

Deerfield was soon after this disaster deserted by the inhabitants, and the Indians reduced the settlement to ashes.

On the 17th of May, 1676, Captain Turner marched from Hatfield at the head of about one hundred and sixty militia-men, to attack a large Indian force stationed at the Great Falls, so called, on Connecticut River, in that part of Deerfield which is now Gill. The Indians had a large settlement there, as it was a famous resort for salmon, bass, and shad. They had at that time a force there of several hundred men. Captain Turner was from Boston, and he commanded the standing forces ; the volunteers were commanded by Captain Holyoke of Springfield, Ensign Lyman of Northampton, and Sergeants Kellogg and Dickinson of Hadley. The Rev. Hope Atherton accompanied them. Benjamin Wait and Experience Hinsdale were pilots. I like to be particular, for I think the names of those who have fought and bled for us should be transmitted to posterity.

There was another party of Indians at this time at Smead's Island, a little more than a mile below. After the defeat of Lathrop and the desertion of Deerfield, the Indians considered themselves in little danger of an attack from the English ; especially as their forces were not numerous at Hadley and the adjacent towns ; they therefore took little pains to protect themselves. In addition to this, two boys who had previously been taken by the Indians on the river below, by the names of Gillet and Stebbins, escaped from them, and informed the English of the situation of their enemies.

This company, well mounted, and under the immediate command of Captain Turner, passed directly through Deerfield Street, which was a short time before in smoking ruins, and across the river at Cheapside, about two miles above, where there was a lodge of Indians, by whom they were heard as they forded the river. They got up and examined the crossing-place, but finding no evidence of horses having passed, they supposed that the noise proceeded from moose crossing the river, and retired to rest. Turner now proceeded to Greenfield Meadow and passed Green River, and continued his route through pathless woods for about four miles, and came to a halt on the west bank of Fall River, where it empties into the Connecticut, about half a mile from the Indian camp above the falls. They here tied their horses, and left them in charge of a small sentry. It was now near day-break, but the Indians were asleep, not even guarded by a single sentinel. It is said they had been rioting the evening before upon milk and roast-beef, which they had stolen from the neighboring towns. The English silently broke in upon their camp, and poured in a charge of musketry which almost completely deafened them. In their consternation and alarm they ran towards the river, crying out, " Mohawks! Mohawks!" supposing themselves attacked by these Indians. Great numbers jumped into their canoes, and many forgot their paddles, and were hurried precipitately over the falls, dashed to pieces, and drowned, while others were de-

7

His horse was shot under him, and the Indians attempted to seize him. He shot the foremost with one of his pistols, which deterred the others from the attempt, and with the assistance of one of his men, who ran to his relief, he escaped from them. A captive at this time informed the English that King Philip was in the pursuit of them with an army of one thousand men. This, with the severe fighting in which they had just been engaged, alarmed them, and they separated into parties, and arranged themselves under different leaders. The enemy were protected and covered by a thick morass, or swamp, extending from the foot of the hill at the falls, nearly to Green River on the west and southwest. One of the parties was cut off by the Indians at the swamp, and another party, having got lost, were taken prisoners by them, and afterwards burnt to death in the Indian manner, which was by covering them with dry bark, setting it on fire, and then quenching it, and kindling it again, until the life of the sufferer was at an end. Captain Turner, who was but just partially recovering from a fit of sickness, with much toil and exertion reached Green River, which as he was passing, the enemy shot him from his horse, and he very soon expired. Captain Holyoke continued his retreat through Green River Meadows, probably across Petty's Plain in Deerfield, and Deerfield Meadows, continually harassed by the Indians, until he reached Hatfield, with the loss of thirty-eight men.

As the detail of individual suffering and personal bravery is always listened to with deep interest and attention, I subjoin the following narration, the substance of which may be found in an attested copy of an account of the sufferings and hardships endured by Mr. Jonathan Wells of Hatfield, in this expedition, a youth then in the seventeenth year of his age, but who became afterwards much esteemed in public life, and who lived to a good old age, honored and beloved by his fellow-townsmen.

Mr. Wells belonged to one of the parties who were under the necessity of contending with the Indians for the possession and recovery of their horses. He was fired upon by three Indians, after he had mounted his horse, and severely wounded; one of the balls whizzed through his hair, another wounded his horse, and a third struck his thigh at a place where it had formerly been fractured by a cart-wheel passing over it. The ball did not entirely break the bone over anew, but merely fractured the end of one of the bones which projected over the other, it having been unskilfully managed at the time it was first set, or reduced. It was with great difficulty, after receiving this wound, that he could retain his seat in the saddle. The Indians, seeing he was wounded, pursued him with great spirit. As soon as he began to recover a little from the shock of the wound, he saw the Indians pressing hard upon him, and, immediately presenting his gun towards them, he held them at bay, and when they again charged upon him, he had the good fortune to escape from them, and to reach his companions. He begged of Captain Turner to go back to the relief of his friends in the rear, as they were exposed to imminent danger from the Indians, or to tarry till they might overtake them. But Turner, probably thinking that self-preservation was the first law of nature, and being himself, with his little band, most critically situated, replied, "It is better to lose some than all." The army now separated into little squads, one leader crying, "If you will save your lives, follow me"; and another, "If you regard your safety, follow me." Mr. Wells followed a party whose course was towards a swamp, but perceiving that a body of the enemy was in that direction, he shifted his course, and fell in with another party, whose route was in a different direction. It was fortunate for him that he did so, for the party which he first joined were all killed by the Indians. His horse soon failed him, on account of the wound which he had received, and he himself was much debilitated from loss of blood, and was not able to keep up with this party, but was left by them, with only one companion, a man by the name of Jones, who was also wounded. The country through which they had to pass was a pathless forest, and they had no guide to direct their course. Mr. Wells was very soon separated from his companion, who, on account of his wounds, was not able to go on with him. At this time he was very faint, and happening to have a nutmeg in his pocket, he ate it, and revived. He wandered about the woods for a considerable time, and by accident arrived upon the banks of Green River, which he followed up to a place called the Country Farms. After having passed the river, in attempting to rise a mountain on the west side of it, he became faint, and fell from his horse. He lay in this situation for a considerable time, but when he came to his senses, his horse was still standing beside him, and the bridle-reins were on his hands. He got up and tied his horse to a tree, and again lay down. Upon more mature reflection, finding himself so extremely debilitated, he thought he should have no further use for his horse ; he humanely let him loose to seek a living for himself in the forest. He unfortunately did not think to take provisions from his portmanteau, which at that time contained an abundance. In the evening he built a fire to keep off the mosquitos, which were very troublesome to him. This came very near destroying him, for the flames spread with so much rapidity among the leaves and underbrush, that, in his faint and exhausted situation, he had great difficulty in escaping from them. He no sooner considered himself out of danger on this account, than he again laid himself down to rest. But new anticipations alarmed him. He feared the Indians would perceive his fire and direct their course towards him, and either kill or captivate him. He had a quantity of ammunition with him, which he was determined should not fall into their hands. After reserving a round or two for his own use, in case of an emergency, he cast the rest of it from him, to a great distance. After having waited a considerable time, and perceiving that the flames had extended themselves over a considerable territory, he began to be encouraged, and filled his wounds with tow, for lint, bound them up with his pocket-handkerchief, and laid down to sleep. During his slumbers he dreamed that his grandfather appeared to him, and informed him that he had strayed out of the right course to Hatfield, and that he must direct his course down the river, and pursue that direction till he came to the termination of a mountain, where there was an extensive plain, on which he must continue his travels until he arrived home. It is very singular that he did not at first go down the river, instead of following it up, as he must have known, if he had reflected a moment, that this was the right direction to Deerfield Street and Hatfield. Upon awaking he felt himself stronger, his wounds had ceased bleeding, and, making use of his gun as a staff, he was able slowly to walk. When he perceived the rising sun the next morning, he was satisfied that he had wandered from his course, and upon observation he concluded that he was now farther from home than he was when at the falls, the place of action. His first thought was to pay no attention to his dream, but, after taking all these things into consideration, he concluded to be governed by it. There was nothing supernatural in this dream. His sleep was probably disturbed, but not so much so that he could not reflect that this must be the natural course for him to pursue. He therefore travelled down the river, and came to the end of the mountain, and soon arrived upon the plain, where he immediately found a foot-path which conducted him to the road where his companions had previously returned. Upon his arrival at Deerfield River, he struggled with great difficulty in passing it, the stream being so powerful as to throw his lame leg over the other, and prevent his wading it. Several of his first efforts were entirely unavailing. However, still using his gun as a staff, he at length succeeded in reaching the opposite shore. Upon rising the bank, being much exhausted, he lay down under a walnut sapling, and fell asleep. On awaking, he perceived an Indian in a ca-

bath he had not advanced any farther than Muddy-Brook, about five miles from the town plat. Here he discovered a human head, probably of one of Lathrop's soldiers, who was killed there the autumn before, which had been dug up by beasts of prey. Notwithstanding his distressed situation, he sought for and found the grave, and laid the head with the body, and covered it with billets of wood in the best manner he was able, to protect it from wild beasts. Upon leaving the brook, and entering upon the plain, he became very faint and thirsty, but could get no water for some time. He, however, was frequently refreshed by holding his face in the smoke of burning pine-knots, which he often found, as the woods had been on fire. This was a frequent custom of the inhabitants in those days, to enable them to pursue their game with greater facility, and to give more free access to their cattle in feeding. He arrived home at noon on the Sabbath, and was received with great joy by his friends, who believed him to be dead. He suffered extremely from his wounds, and many times afterwards was confined to his bed for six months at a time. It was more than four years before he entirely recovered.

The following is an extract of a sermon delivered by the Rev. Mr. Atherton, pastor of the church at Hatfield. Mr. Atherton was in this action, and the sermon was delivered on the Sabbath after his return: — "In the hurry and confusion of the retreat, I was separated from the army. The night following I wandered up and down among the dwelling-places of the enemy, but none of them discovered me. The next day I tendered myself to them a prisoner, for no way of escape appeared, and I had been a long time without food ; but notwithstanding I offered myself to them, yet they accepted not my offer; when I spoke, they answered not ; and when I moved towards them, they fled. Finding they would not accept of me as a prisoner, I determined to take the course of the river, and, if possible, find the way home ; and after several days of hunger, fatigue, and danger, I reached Hatfield."

The Indians were very superstitious with regard to priests or ministers of the Gospel, believing them to be supernatural beings. This may account for their conduct to Mr. Atherton at this time.

The government of Massachusetts, in compensation for the services of Captains Turner and Holyoke and their men in this engagement, granted them and their successors the township called Bernardston, then Falltown.*

The following year, 1677, an attempt was made to resettle the town. Very soon after, however, a number of the people were slain, and the town was deserted. A man by the name of John Root was killed on the 19th of September of this year, and three others, by the names of Sergeant Plympton, Quintin Stockwell, and Benoni Stebbins, were taken prisoners. Stebbins escaped and returned to Deerfield, Plympton was burnt at the stake, and it is said that the Indians compelled a Mr. Dickinson to lead him to it, and that he went to it with cheerfulness. In the year 1682 the settlers returned, and for several years were unmolested by the Indians. This year the town of Deerfield was incorporated.

* See Appendix and Notes.

At the time of the additional grant of the Legislature to the eight thousand acres, in the year 1673, so as to constitute Pocomptuck a township of an area of seven square miles, one of the conditions of the grant was, that the inhabitants should settle an orthodox minister within three years. The settlements on Connecticut River were at that time, and for a long time afterwards, in a state of continual jeopardy from savage warfare and Indian incursions. The great battles of Lathrop and Turner had paralyzed the enterprise of the pioneers of the wilderness, and it was a long time before they recovered their energies. It was not till the year 1682 that any great efforts were made at re-settlement. A few inhabitants returned that year, and for several succeeding years they were not much molested by the Indians. On account of these disturbances, the town did not comply with the conditions of the grant, yet no exceptions were taken by the government. On the contrary, additional grants were afterwards made to the limits of the town.

In March, 1686, Mr. Williams was ordained the first minister of the Gospel in Deerfield, when he was but little more than twenty-one years of age. He must have been shielded by the whole armor of the Christian warfare, to have risked his life in so hazardous an undertaking. The following is the agreement between him and his people, copied from the early records of the town.

"The inhabitants of Deerfield, to encourage Mr. John Williams to settle amongst them, to dispense the blessed word of truth unto them, have made propositions to him as followeth : —

"That they will give him sixteen cow-commons of meadow land, with a home-lot that lieth on the meeting-house hill; — that they will build him a house forty-two feet long, twenty feet wide, with a lento on the back side of the house, to finish said house, to fence his home-lot, and, within two years after this agreement, to build him a barn, and break up his ploughing land. For yearly salary, to give him sixty pounds a year for the present, and four or five years after this agreement, to add to his salary, and make it eighty pounds.

"The committee approved and ratified the above propositions on the condition Mr. Williams settle among them.

"Attest, Medad Pumry, by order of the committee."

"At a meeting of the inhabitants of Deerfield, December 17, 1686, there was granted to Mr. John Williams a certain piece of land lying within the meadow fence, beginning at Joseph Sheldon's north line, and so runs to Deerfield River, north, or northeast, the owners of the common fence maintaining it as it now is at the time of the grant."

There was a further agreement between Mr. Williams and the town in relation to his salary, in 1696 – 7 : —

"The town to pay their salary to me in wheat, pease, Indian corn, and pork, at the prices stated; viz. wheat at 3s. 3d. per bushel, Indian corn at 2s. per bushel, fatted pork at 2½d. per lb., these being the terms of the bargain made with me at the first.

(Signed,)   "John Williams."

About seven years after his settlement, on the 6th of June, 1693, Indian depredations again commenced at Deerfield, and the widow Hepzibah Wells, of his society, and three of her daughters, were knocked down and scalped, one of whom recovered from the terrific maiming. Thomas Broughton and his wife and three children were also killed at the same time. A few months afterwards, a man by the name of Martin Smith was taken prisoner and carried to Canada, but he returned in a few years.

The fort at Deerfield was again attacked on the 16th of September, 1694, by Monsieur Castreen, and an Indian force under his command. The attack was unsuccessful, but a boy by the name of Daniel Severance was killed in the meadows, and two soldiers by the names of Beaumont and Richard Lyman were wounded in the fort. A schoolmistress by the name of Mrs. Hannah Beaumont and her scholars were almost miraculously preserved ; being fired upon by the Indians as they ran from the house to the fort, the bullets whistled about their ears, but not one of them was in the least injured, although the Indians were very near them.

As Mr. Joseph Barnard and a party of our men were on their return from Hatfield on the 18th of August, 1695, they were attacked by a party of Indians who had concealed themselves beneath a bridge in the south meadows about two miles south of the street, on the road leading to the Bars. Barnard himself was badly wounded in his body and in both hands ; his horse was shot under him, and fell dead. Through the instrumentality and courage of Godfry Nims, he was rescued from the enemy and brought to the fort at Deerfield, where he lived to the 6th of September, when he died, greatly lamented. The oldest monument which we can now find in our old burying-ground is erected to his memory, bearing date 1695. The bridge is still in the same situation, across the brook where Mr. Barnard fell, as it was then, and it is called Indian Bridge.

On the 16th of September, 1696, as two men, by the names of Thomas Smead and John Gillet, were out from the fort hunting, up Green River, towards the north part of the present town of Greenfield, they were attacked, and Gillet was captured by the Indians. Smead was so fortunate as to make his escape.

The Indians now made a rapid advance to the fort at Deerfield village, and took Mr. Daniel Belding and a son and daughter (Nathaniel and Esther). They also killed his wife and three children, and wounded two other children. They both recovered, although the son had his skull fractured by an Indian tomahawk, and a portion of brain issued from the wound.

In July, 1698, a man by the name of Nathaniel Pomroy was killed by the enemy, as he was out in pursuit of some Indians up the river, who had been committing depredations at Hatfield. General Hoyt, in his Antiquarian Researches, gives this account of the transaction : — " About the middle of July, a short time before sunset, a small party of Indians killed a man and boy in Hatfield Meadows, on the banks of Connecticut River, and captured two lads, Samuel Dickinson, and one Charley ; they put them on board of canoes and proceeded up the river. The intelligence being received at Deerfield, thirteen miles above, twelve men were detached to that place to incercept the Indians. Proceeding about twenty miles, they selected a favorable spot on the right bank of the river, and lay till morning, when they discovered the Indians coming up near the opposite bank with the captured lads, in two canoes. Carefully marking their objects, the whole party gave the Indians an unexpected fire, by which one was wounded. The others, with one of the lads, leaped from the canoes and gained the shore. They then attempted to kill the lads, but receiving another well-directed fire, they fell back; on which the lad on the shore joined his companion in the canoe, and both escaped across the river to their deliverers. Five or six of the party then embarked with the design of seizing the other canoe, which at this time had lodged at an island a little below. Two Indians who lay secreted not far distant fired and killed Nathaniel Pomroy, one of the party. The Indians then retired into the woods, and the English returned to Deerfield. The place where this exploit happened is a short distance above the mouth of Ashuelot River, where the Connecticut makes a remarkable flexure at the present town of Vernon, in Vermont."

In the year 1699 the town ordered the pickets round the old fort to be repaired. Heavy penalties were annexed for the non-fulfilment of these orders. The pickets were probably commenced by our people in King Philip's war, which began about the year 1689. At the time the orders of the town were issued, they were considerably out of repair. At a time of savage warfare and Indian incursions, these precautions were absolutely necessary. These pickets included about

twenty acres, and the old house was inclosed near the
northwest angle of them.   Many dwelling-houses were
at the same time rudely fortified, by being surrounded
with cleft or round sticks of timber placed erect in the
ground, and the walls were lined with bricks, which
were considered to be musket-proof, — a very insecure
mode of protection, even against savages.

On the 8th of October, 1703, two prisoners were
taken from Deerfield, in the meadows, near Brough-
ton's Pond, at or near the north end of the street, by
the names of Zebediah Williams and John Nims, and
carried to Canada.   Nims escaped with some other
prisoners, and after much fatigue and danger returned
to Deerfield.   Williams died in Canada.

Let us now pause for a moment, and contrast our
situation at the present day with that of our unhappy
ancestors, who have toiled and bled to transmit to us
this rich inheritance, these beautiful domains.   We are
now in peace and security, enjoying the blessings of
rational liberty, and surrounded by all which can make
life desirable.   The country is densely inhabited; our
roads are good, and intelligence can be conveyed to
the remotest quarters in a short space of time.   We
are in no danger of invasion from a foreign or a do-
mestic foe.   We need no muskets to protect us while
at labor in our fields, no guards to defend us during
the silent watches of the night.   The blood of our sons
no longer fattens our cornfields; no savage war-whoop
awakens the sleep of our cradles.   Our firesides are
our altars, and we can enjoy them unmolested.   How
different was the case with our forefathers !   The
country was new; it was infested with savages thirst-

ing for blood.   Their population was thin, confined
to a few villages, and the inhabitants of these had as
much as they could do to defend themselves from
Indian barbarities.   Few roads but bridle and foot-
paths, and all attempts to convey information, and all
calls for succor, tedious and slow, at the imminent haz-
ard of an ambuscade or life. Self-preservation was the
first and only law. It was unsafe to go into a neigh-
bor's house without a musket, much more into the field.
Their houses were within the rude walls of a picket-
ed fort, and almost the only communication between
them was by means of passages under ground from
cellar to cellar. Sentinels always guarded their houses
by night. It was a state of continual jeopardy, and in
the country of an implacable and vindictive savage
foe. No succors could be received from government;
every thing depended upon individual exertion. Such
was the situation of our fathers in this town on the
eventful morning of the 29th of February, old style,
1704.

The names of several of the captives who were
taken from Deerfield, and who were left in Canada
after Mr. Williams's return, have been found among
the Indians near Montreal.   There were several inter-
marriages, and their names have not become extinct
in that vicinity. As lately as the year 1756, Mary
Harris, who was one of the female prisoners, and a
child at the time of the capture of the town, resided at
Cahnawaga. She was at that time a married woman,
and had several children, one of whom was an officer
in the service of France. A gentleman from Montreal
said that he saw, at the Lake of the Two Mountains, a

French girl, who told him that her grandmother was
Thankful Stebbins, who was taken from Deerfield in
1704. General Hoyt has procured the names of the
principal part of the prisoners who were taken at Deer-
field, and who were left in Canada after the return of
Mr. Williams. They are as follows: —

William Brooks, Mary Brooks, Daniel Crowfoot,
Samuel Carter, John Carter, Mary Carter, Elizabeth
Corse, Abigail Denio, Mary Field, Freedom French,
Abigail French, Mary Harris, Samuel Hastings, Eb-
enezer Hoit, Thomas Hurst, Joanna Kellog, Abigail
Nims, Jeremiah Richards, Josiah Rising, Ebenezer
Stebbins, Thankful Stebbins, Joseph Stebbins, Eliza-
beth Stevens, Waitstill Warner, Eunice Williams.

Many of the prisoners became very much attached
to the Indians and their mode of life, and some of
them were very loath to leave them after they were re-
deemed. A lad, by the name of Jonathan Hoit, who
was taken at the time of the destruction of the town, at
the age of sixteen years, was very fond of them. He
resided with them two years and a half, at a place
called Lorette, upon the River St. Charles, not far
from Quebec. He learnt their language so perfectly,
that he never forgot it to the day of his death, which
was in the ninety-second year of his age. Soon after
his return to Deerfield, his former Indian master came
down to make him a visit, and he was kindly received
by him, and treated with respect. Jonathan was re-
deemed by Major Dudley, son of Governor Dudley, of
Massachusetts, in the following manner, as related by
Colonel Elihu Hoyt, one of his descendants, in his
History of the First Settlement of Deerfield, — a small
pamphlet in a duodecimo form.

" The Indians were in the habit of raising and bring-
ing to market garden sauce, &c. One day Major
Dudley saw young Hoit in the street; he said to him,
' Are you not an English boy ? ' He answered, ' Yes.'
' Do you not wish to go home and see your friends ? '
' I do,' was the answer. ' Where is your master ? '
said the Major. ' Somewhere in the city,' answered
the boy. ' Bring him to me,' said he. The boy now
tripped over the ground with a light heart, in pursuit
of his master, who soon came. The agent said to the
Indian, ' I will give you this for the boy,' holding out
to him a purse of twenty dollars. The temptation was
too great to be resisted ; the bargain was made, the
money handed over, and the Indian went away well
satisfied. The gentleman immediately sent the boy
on board a ship then lying in the river for the recep-
tion of the ransomed prisoners. The agent was aware
that, when the Indian had leisure to reflect, he would
return and make a proposition to give up the money,
and take his boy again. He was not mistaken in his
conjecture ; he soon came back, and desired to give up
the money for the boy ; but was told he could not have
him, for he was out of his reach. The Indian went
away lamenting that he had parted with his favorite
captive boy for a few dumb dollars, that would neither
fish nor hunt. By this means the captive was restored
to his home and his friends."

About the time that Mr. Williams left Canada, new
troubles began to arise in that Province. Letters were
received from Mississippi, written in the preceding
May, stating that the plague was prevailing there, and
that one hundred and fifty Frenchmen had died within

a very short space of time, and that the tribe of Indians there called the Lazilouways were very boisterous, and had wounded a Jesuit severely, and had killed his servant, a Frenchman.   Farther information reached them in July, that the Indians upon the river were engaged in war with each other, and the French who resided amongst them were in great danger; that the Mitchel Macquinas had commenced war against the Miziamnies, and killed a friar, three Frenchmen, and eleven Indians, at a place called the Straits, where they were erecting a fort for the purpose of traffic; they had also taken sixteen Frenchmen prisoners, and burned their trading-houses.   These things greatly perplexed the French in Canada; the Jesuits strove hard to pacify them, but their troubles rather increased than subsided when they left Canada; for the last letters from the French prisoners in those regions state that the Indians had sent out two companies, one of one hundred and sixty, and one of one hundred and fifty-nine, against the savages at the Straits, and they were fearful that they would attack the French as well as the Indians.

Mr. Williams did not immediately return to Deerfield after his emancipation from the French and Indians.   He probably had some doubts whether he should again settle in the ministry in Deerfield.   On the 30th of November, 1706, nine or ten days after his arrival at Boston, the town chose commissioners, viz. "Captain Thomas French and Captain Jonathan Wells, to go down to the bay for them, and in their behalf to act and treat with their pastor, the Rev. John Williams, in order to his re-settlement with them again in the

work of the ministry, as also to take advice and coun-
sel of the elders in our county for the management of
the work, as also to put up a petition to the General
Court, or Council, for a grant of money for the en-
couragement of the Rev. Mr. John Williams in his re-
settlement in said work with them, and in all these
particulars to act and do according to the best of their
discretion." Mr. Williams, after serious consideration,
accepted the call, although the war still continued with
unabated fury, and the inhabitants were kept in a con-
tinual state of alarm.

On the 9th of January, 1707, the town agreed to
build a house for him, " as big as Ensign Sheldon's,
and a back room as big as may be thought conven-
ient." Ensign Sheldon's house was the old picketed
fort,* which was recently torn down. On the 3d of
April the town voted, " that they would pay unto Mr.
John Williams 20 pounds in money, and every male
head of 16 years and upwards, one day's work a
piece ; those that have teams, a day with their teams
for the year." They also voted " to pay Thomas
Wells for boarding Mr. Choate the last half-year he
preached in Deerfield." On the 17th of November
they voted " to send a petition to the General Court
for a grant of money towards the maintenance of the
Rev. John Williams in the work of the ministry in
Deerfield." They also gave him and his heirs for
ever a large tract of land adjoining his house, and in
the meadows.

Indian depredations continued for many years after

---

* See engraving.

the re-settlement of Mr. Williams. Soon after the destruction of the town at the time he was captivated, the inhabitants rebuilt it. In May, 1704, Mr. John Allen and his wife were killed at a place called the Barrs, and in the summer of the same year, Sergeant John Hawks was attacked by the Indians, but escaped to Hatfield with a slight wound upon his hand; and in July a man by the name of Thomas Russell was killed by them at the north part of the town.

August, 1708. As a scout from Deerfield were returning from White River, in Vermont, they were attacked by the Indians, and a man by the name of Barber was killed, he having killed the Indian who fired upon him, so near together did they discharge their guns. Martin Kellogg was captivated; the rest were so fortunate as to escape. On the 26th of October of this year, Mr. Ebenezer Field was killed by the Indians near Bloody-Brook.

In the month of April, 1709, Mehuman Hinsdale, a son of one of the first settlers of Deerfield, and the first male child ever born there, was taken prisoner by the Indians, as he was driving his team between Hatfield and Northampton, and carried by them to Canada. From thence he was carried to France, and from France to England, and brought from the latter place to Deerfield.* The succeeding month of the same year, Lieutenant John Wells and John Burt, inhabitants of Deerfield, were killed in a skirmish with the Indians on French or Onion River, in Vermont. They, with others, had been out on an expedition against the en-

---

* See Appendix and Notes.

emy, as far as Lake Champlain, where they had killed several of them.

It seems that the Indians and their commanders were not yet satisfied with their hostilities upon this land, abounding with milk and honey, for another attempt was made to sack or destroy the town in the month of June, 1709, by Rouville, one of the brothers who made the successful attack upon the town in 1704. His force consisted of one hundred and eighty French and Indians; but vigorous efforts were now made by the inhabitants for the defence, many of whom had recently returned from Canada, and their late disasters had taught them military prudence, and inspired them with courage in opposing the savage foes. The enemy, from these preparations, thought it most prudent to withdraw their troops and abandon the attack. They did not quit the place until they had taken Joseph Clesson and John Arms prisoners. Jonathan Williams and Matthew Clesson were killed at the time, and Lieutenant Mattoon and Isaac Taylor were wounded, but both of them fortunately survived. I am inclined to think that this Joseph Clesson was the one who was so cruelly treated by the Indians in Canada in one of their sports, which was to cause him to run the gantlet. The account of the transaction is as follows: — The Indians arranged themselves in two rows facing each other, armed with clubs. They then pinioned the hands of the captive, and forced him to run through the ranks, while every Indian gave him a severe blow with his club. Mr. Clesson was severely mangled by them in this way, while in Canada and under the protection of the French. His lower jaw was broken, and he was

otherwise most cruelly bruised. He was ever after-
wards extremely indignant against them for this out-
rage, and the bare mention of an Indian would rouse a
resentment in his breast as furious as a lion in its rage.

Mr. Williams about this time was earnestly solicited
to accept the office of chaplain in the army in the ex-
pedition against Canada under General Hill and Ad-
miral Walker. He had been previously requested to
accept the same in the expedition against Port Royal,
under the command of Colonel March, with seven hun-
dred men, in the year 1707. Soon after, he was ap-
pointed a commissioner in the winter expedition to
Canada, under the command of Colonel Stoddard, for
the purpose of redeeming prisoners. They were suc-
cessful in redeeming many of their fellow-citizens, but
could not obtain the daughter of Mr. Williams.

Mr. Williams's salary was for some time probably
too small to support him, and the General Court al-
lowed him two islands in Connecticut River, opposite
to the town of Deerfield, now called Smead's and
Corse's islands, containing between thirty and forty
acres, in consequence of his petitioning on behalf of
the town for an extension of its territories. This peti-
tion was granted, and the line then extended west from
Connecticut River nine miles, as far as the western
boundaries of Northampton and Hatfield. The town
was then about fourteen miles in length and nine in
breadth, and occupied the towns now embracing
Greenfield, Conway, Shelburne, Gill, and a part of
Whately.

On the 30th of September, 1712, a scout was sent
from Deerfield, under the command of Samuel Taylor,

to the Hudson or North River, as it was then called, in the State of New York. They were attacked by the Indians on this day, and a man by the name of Samuel Andros was killed; Jonathan Barret was wounded, and he and William Stanford were taken prisoners, carried to Canada, and redeemed by Lieutenant Samuel Williams, who was there with a flag of truce, and they returned to Deerfield after an absence of two months. From the year 1712 to 1720, the people of Deerfield were not much molested by the Indians.

To show the continued attachment of the people of Deerfield to Mr. Williams, the town voted to provide him his wood at its own expense, in addition to his salary, and to procure him the value of sixty ordinary loads in the year 1724 – 5.

In the latter part of June, 1724, as a scout were returning from the north part of Greenfield, near Rocky Mountain, to the fort at Deerfield, they were attacked by the Indians, and Ebenezer Sheldon, Thomas Colton, and Jeremiah English, a friendly Indian, were killed. The Indians were dispersed by the rear of the scout coming upon them suddenly. In the same year two men, by the names of Lieutenant Timothy Childs and Samuel Allen, who had been at work in the North Meadows, were attacked by a party of Indians who lay concealed in the woods at Pine Hill. They were both wounded, but fortunately recovered.

On the 25th of August, 1725, as Deacon Field, Deacon Childs, and several others from Deerfield, were passing up the road near Green River Farms, they were ambuscaded by the Indians, whom the party had previously discovered, as they were posted on an eminence. An Indian was killed by John Wells. The party afterwards returned towards a mill, but one of them, Deacon Field, was severely wounded, the ball passing through the lower part of the right side of the abdomen, cutting off several folds of the mesentery, which protruded through the wound to the extent of two inches, and was cut off even with the body. The ball then passed between the two lowest ribs, fracturing the last one. It likewise took off one of his thumbs at the root, and the bone of the forefinger, and lodged in the hand between the fore and second finger. The ball was extracted, and a perfect cure of all his wounds was effected, by Dr. Thomas Hastings, in less than three weeks.

Mr. Williams for many years devoted much of his time and attention to the pursuits of science and literature, added to the cares and obligations attendant upon his professional duties as a faithful minister of the Gospel. For the times in which he lived, he was a writer of no mean abilities. He has not left behind him many of his published productions. I recollect only to have seen his " Redeemed Captive returning to Zion," in which he gives an account of his captivity and sufferings, and a Sermon preached at Boston, December 6, 1706, soon after his return from Canada. These works evince talent and great piety. The age in which he lived was not one of publications like the present, or doubtless more of his works would have been published. He was a very constant attendant upon the annual convention of ministers in the then Province at Boston, when he was always treated with respect and attention. In 1728 he preached an interesting discourse at that convention.

I have seen some of his manuscript productions, which are interesting. In some of his writings, under the head of Philosophy, he treats of Mists and Fogs, — of Wind, — of Water, or the Doctrine of Hydrostatics, — of Matter, — of the Earth, — of Fire, — of Beasts, Birds, and Fishes, — of Insects, — of the Julian Period, — of the Method of Drawing a Meridian Line upon an Horizontal Plane, — of Mercury, — of Vulcan, — of Mars, — of an Echo, &c., &c. These topics show that he had a philosophical turn of mind, and a greater taste for the abstruse sciences than is usual to be found at that period.

The following is his description of a drunkard, which will give some idea of his style of writing, and will show that the habit of intoxication is not confined to the present day : —

"A DRUNKARD DESCRIBED.

"Though wine is so beneficial to this life, that *in vitæ vitam hominis Esseidieros*, and how many say that the happiness of one consists in the enjoyment of the other; but do not consider that, if wine be the cradle of life, yet it is the grave of the reason, for if men do not constantly sail in the Red Sea of claret, their souls are ofttimes drowned therein. It blinds them, and leaves them under darkness, especially when it begins to draw forth sparkles and little stars from their eyes. Then the body being drowned in drink, the mind floats, or else is stranded. Thus too great love of the vine is pernicious to life, for from it come more faults than grapes, and it breeds more mischief than pleasures. Would you see an instance of this, observe

a drunken man.   O beast! — see how his head reels
and totters, his hands sink, his feet fail, his hands
tremble, his mouth froths, his cheeks are flabby, his
eyes sparkle and water, his words are unintelligible,
his tongue falters and stops, his throat sends forth a
nasty, loathsome stench! — But what do I do?   There
is no end to his filthiness."

Soon after Mr. Williams's return to Deerfield, he
was married, a second time, to the daughter of Captain
Allen of Windsor, Connecticut.   She, as well as his
first wife, were granddaughters of the Rev. Mr. War-
ham, formerly pastor of Windsor.   By his second wife
he had five children.   Eight of his children survived
him, four sons and four daughters.   His three eldest
sons, Eleazer, Stephen, and Warham, were settled in
the ministry at Mansfield, Conn., at Springfield, and at
Watertown, Mass.   Stephen received the degree of
Doctor of Divinity from Dartmouth College, but was
educated at Harvard.   He lived to a great old age.
His son Elijah, by his second wife, was educated at
Harvard College, and lived at Deerfield, where he was
much respected as an honorable merchant and an able
magistrate.   His eldest daughter married Mr. Meacham,
the former pastor of Coventry, Conn.

Mr. Williams died at Deerfield on the 12th of June,
1729, in the sixty-fifth year of his age and the forty-
fourth of his ministry.   He was attacked with a fit of
apoplexy on the morning of the 9th.   It was perceived
upon speaking to him, that he had the exercise of
reason, but he was never able to articulate distinctly
more than two or three words after he was taken ill.

The writer of his obituary notice, which was published in the Boston News-Letter, the first newspaper ever printed in New England, thus speaks of him : —

"God, who first sent him to us, and inclined his heart to settle with us in our small beginnings, hath made him a great blessing unto us. His heart was engaged in his work, and was abundant in his labors, both in season and out of season, plainly, faithfully, and frequently warning, urging, and entreating both elder and younger unto piety and perseverance in it. He was much in prayer, and singularly gifted in it. We hope through grace he has left many seals of his ministry among us. The Divine Providence which fixed his post in one of the frontier towns of the Province, fitted him for it by giving him patience and cheerfulness of spirit; so that he was wonderfully carried through all the difficulties, distractions, and dangers that he encountered. And his prayers, counsel, and example did not a little contribute to the support and encouragement of his people from time to time."

And another writer, the Rev. Rodolphus Dickinson, of this town, in his View of Deerfield, thus beautifully eulogizes him : —

"The character of Mr. Williams was extensively known, and held in high estimation; as may be learned, aside from other respectful attentions, by his appointment to preach to a general convention of the clergymen of Massachusetts at Boston. He is represented by his contemporaries, who have witnessed his efforts before the most enlightened and powerful auditories in the Province, as a powerful and affecting preacher. He is also commended for his domestic

virtues, his eminent piety, humility, sincerity, and
goodness of heart. His voluntary abandonment of the
scenes of his beloved nativity, secure from the incur-
sions of the savages, to settle in a frontier place, per-
petually opposed to their depredations, where personal
safety, so indispensable to other enjoyments, was for
many years a stranger to their habitations, and his re-
turn to the work of the ministry, subject to the same
dangers, after the complicated afflictions of his captiv-
ity, evince his ardent love for the people of his care,
and testify that he was animated with the spirit of a
martyr in the advancement of the Gospel. It is im-
possible to peruse his interesting narrative of the de-
struction of Deerfield, and the slaughter and captivity
of its inhabitants, in the suffering in which he so large-
ly participated, without being inspired with a respect
for his talents and piety, and an admiration of that un-
exampled fortitude which could sustain him under pri-
vate calamities such as rarely happen to man, and a
view of public desolations, similar, though less extend-
ed, to those apostrophized by the mournful son of Hil-
kiah. But a holy resignation to the Supreme Disposer
of events was the balm of every sorrow. His path
was lighted by a hope that looks beyond this transient
scene. He was redeemed from the flames, passed
through the wilderness and sea of dangers, and, as we
trust, reached a temple eternal in the heavens."

APPENDIX AND NOTES.

List of the Soldiers and the Descendants of such as are deceased that were in the Fight, called the Fall Fight, above Deerfield, who are entitled to the Township granted by the General Court, as follows :—

Joseph Atherton, Deerfield, only son of Hope Atherton.
Nathaniel Allexander, Northampton, Nathaniel Allexander.
Thomas Alvard, Middleton, eldest son of Thomas Alvard.
John Arms, Deerfield, son of William Arms.
John Baker, Northampton, son of Timothy Baker.
Samuel Bedortha, Springfield, son of Samuel Bedortha.
John Field, Deerfield, descendant, James Bennet.
John Barbar, Springfield, son of John Barbar.
John Bradshaw, Medford, John Bradshaw.
Isaac Burnap, Windham, son of John Burnap.
Samuel Clesson, Northampton, descendant, Peter Bushrod.
Samuel Boltwood, Hadley, son of Samuel Boltwood.
Samuel Bardwell, Deerfield, son of Robert Bardwell.
John Hitchcock, Springfield, descendant, Samuel Ball.
Stephen Belden, Hatfield, son of Stephen Belden.
Richard Beers, Watertown, son of Elnathan Beers.
Samuel Beldin, Hatfield, Samuel Beldin.
Preserved Clapp, Northampton, son of Preserved Clapp.
Thomas Chapin, Springfield, son of Japhet Chapin.
Samuel Crow, Hadley, son of Samuel Crow.
Joseph Crowfoot, Wethersfield, descendant, Joseph Crowfoot.

William Clark, Lebanon, son of William Clark.
Noah Cook, Hadley, descendant, Noah Colman.
Benjamin Chamberlain, Colchester, Benjamin Chamberlain.
Nathaniel Chamberlain, descendant, Joseph Chamberlain.
Samuel Cuniball, Boston, son of John Cuniball.
John Chase, Newbury, son of John Chase.
William Dickeson, Hadley, son of Nehemiah Dickeson.
Samuel Jellet, Hatfield, descendant, John Dickeson.
Benjamin Edwards, Northampton, son of Benjamin Edwards.
Joseph Fuller, Newtown, Joseph Fuller.
Samuel Field, Deerfield, son of Samuel Field.
Nathaniel Foot, Colchester, son of Nathaniel Foot.
John Flanders, Kingston, son of John Flanders.
Isaac Gleason, Enfield, son of Isaac Gleason.
Richard Church, Hadley, descendant, Isaac Harrison.
Simon Grover, Malden, son of Simon Grover.
Samuel Griffin, Roxbury, son of Joseph Griffin.
John Hitchcock, Springfield, son of John Hitchcock.
Luke Hitchcock, Springfield, son of Luke Hitchcock.
Jonathan Hoit, Deerfield, son of David Hoit.
Jonathan Scott, Waterbury, descendant, John Hawks.
Eleazer Hawks, Deerfield, son of Eleazer Hawks.
James Harwood, Concord, son of James Harwood.
John Dond, Middleton, descendant, Experience Hindal.
Samuel Hunt, Tewksbury, Samuel Hunt.
William James, Lebanon, son of Abell James.
John Ingram, Hadley, son of John Ingram.
Samuel Jellet, Hatfield, son of Samuel Jellet.
William Jones, Almsbury, son of Robert Jones.
Medad King, Northampton, son of John King.
Francis Keet, Northampton, son of Francis Keet.
Martin Kellog, Suffield, son of Joseph Kellog.
John Lee, Westfield, son of John Lee.
John Lyman, Northampton, son of John Lyman.
Joseph Leeds, Dorchester, son of Joseph Leeds.
Josiah Leonard, Springfield, son of Josiah Leonard.

John Merry, Long Island, son of Cornelius Merry.
Stephen Noble, formerly of Enfield, descendant, Isaac Morgan.
Jonathan Morgan, Springfield, son of Jonathan Morgan.
Thomas Miller, Springfield, son of Thomas Miller.
James Mun, Colchester, James Mun.
Benjamin Mun, Deerfield, son of John Mun.
John Mattoon, Wallingford, son of Philip Mattoon.
John Nims, Deerfield, son of Godfrey Nims.
Ebenezer Pumroy, Northampton, son of Medad Pumroy.
Samuel Pumroy, N. H., son of Caleb Pumroy.
Samuel Price, Glastenbury, son of Robert Price.
Samuel Preston, Hadley, descendant, John Preston.
Thomas Pratt, Malden, son of John Pratt.
John Pressey, Almsbury, son of John Pressey.
Henry Rogers, Springfield, son of Henry Rogers.
John Read, Westford, son of Thomas Read.
Nathaniel Sikes, Springfield, son of Nathaniel Sikes.
Nathaniel Sutliff, Durham, son of Nathaniel Sutliff.
Samuel Stebbins, Springfield, son of Samuel Stebbins.
Luke Noble, Westfield, descendant, Thomas Stebbins.
Ebenezer Smead, Deerfield, son of William Smead.
Joseph Smith, Hatfield, son of John Smith.
James Stephenson, Springfield, son of James Stephenson.
Thomas Seldon, Haddam, son of Joseph Seldon.
Josiah Scott, Hatfield, son of William Scott.
John Salter, Charlestown, son of John Salter.
William Turner, Swanzey, grandson of Captain Turner.
Benjamin Thomas, Strafford, son of Benjamin Thomas.
Joseph Winchell, jr., Suffield, descendant, Jonathan Tailer.
Samuel Tyley, Boston, son of Samuel Tyley.
Preserved Wright, N. H., son of James Wright.
Cornelius Webb, Springfield, son of John Webb.
Jonathan Webb, Stamford, son of Richard Webb.
John Wait, Hatfield, son of Benjamin Wait.
Eleazer Weller, Westfield, son of Eleazer Weller.
Thomas Wells, Deerfield, son of Thomas Wells.

Ebenezer Warriner, Enfield, son of Joseph Warriner.
Jonathan Wells, Deerfield, Jonathan Wells.
Wm. Worthington, Colchester, son Nicholas Worthington.
John Scott, Elbows, grandson of John Scott.
Samuel Colby, Almsbury.
Irgal Newberry, Malden.

> The Committee appointed to enlist the Officers
> and Soldiers in the Fight, called the Fall Fight,
> under the Command of Capt. William Turner,
> then slain, and the Descendants of such as are
> deceased, and that are entitled to the Grant of
> this Great and General Court made them of a
> Township, have attended many times that Ser-
> vice and returned the List above and aforesaid,
> which contains the Person's Names claiming,
> and from whom and which the Committee have
> accordingly allowed, all which is submitted.

A List of yᵉ
Proprietary.

> WM. DUDLEY,
> EZ. LEWIS,
> JOHN STODDARD,
> JOSEPH DWIGHT,
> JOHN WAINWRIGHT.

Boston, June, 1736.

In Council, June 23d, 1736, Read, and ordered that this
Report be accepted.   Sent down for Concurrence :
SIMON FROST, *Dept'y Sec'ry.*

In the House of Representatives, Jan'y 19, 1736, Read,
and ordered that this Report be accepted.   Sent up for Con-
currence.   J. QUINCY, *Spk'r.*

In Council, Jan'y 21st, 1736, Read and Concurr'd.
SIMON FROST, *Dept'y Sec'ry.*

Consented to,   J. BELCHER.

A true Copy, Examin'd pr. SIMON FROST, *Dept. Sec'ry.*

Names of the Captives who were taken at the Destruction of the Town of Deerfield, February 29th, 1703-4. Drawn up by the Rev. Stephen Williams, of Springfield, soon after his Return from Captivity.

Mary Alexander.

Mary Alexander, jr.

Joseph Alexander, (ran away the first night.)

Sarah Allen.

Mary Allis.

Thomas Baker.

Simon Beaumont.

Hepzibah Belding.*

John Bridgman, (ran away in the meadow.)

Nathaniel Brooks.

Mary Brooks.*

Mary Brooks, jr.

William Brooks.

Abigail Brown.

Benjamin Burt.

Hannah Carter.*

Hannah Carter, jr.*

Mercy Carter.

Samuel Carter.

John Carter.

Ebenezer Carter.

Marah Carter.*

John Catlin.

Ruth Catlin.

Elizabeth Corse.*

Elizabeth Corse, jr.

Daniel Crowfoot.

Abigail Denio.

Sarah Dickinson.

Joseph Eastman.

Mary Field.

John Field.

Mary Field, jr.

Mary Frary.*

Thomas French.

Mary French.*

Mary French, jr.

Thomas French, jr.

Freedom French.

Martha French.

Abigail French.

Mary Harris.

Samuel Hastings.

Elizabeth Hawks.

Mehuman Hinsdale.

Mary Hinsdale.

Jacob Hicks, (died at Coos.)

Deacon David Hoit, (died at Coos.)

Abigail Hoit.

Jonathan Hoit.

Sarah Hoit.

---

* This mark designates those who were slain in the meadows after they left the town.

Ebenezer Hoit.

Abigail Hoit, jr.

Elizabeth Hull.

Thomas Hurst.

Ebenezer Hurst.

Benoni Hurst.*

Sarah Hurst.

Sarah Hurst, jr.

Elizabeth Hurst.

Hannah Hurst.

Martin Kellogg.

Martin Kellogg, jr.

Joseph Kellogg.

Joanna Kellogg.

Rebecca Kellogg.

John Marsh.

Sarah Mattoon.*

Philip Mattoon.

Frank,* (a negro.)

Mehitable Nims.

Ebenezer Nims.

Abigail Nims.

Joseph Petty.

Sarah Petty.

Lydia Pomeroy.

Joshua Pomeroy.

Esther Pomeroy.*

Samuel Price.

Jemima Richards.

Josiah Rising.

Hannah Shelden.

Ebenezer Shelden.

Remembrance Shelden.

Mary Shelden.

John Stebbins.

Dorothy Stebbins.

John Stebbins, jr.

Samuel Stebbins.

Ebenezer Stebbins.

Joseph Stebbins.

Thankful Stebbins.

Elizabeth Stevens.

Ebenezer Warner,

Waitstill Warner, jr.*

Sarah Warner.

Rev. John Williams.

Mrs. Eunice Williams.*

Samuel Williams.

Stephen Williams.

Eunice Williams, jr.

Esther Williams.

Warham Williams.

John Weston.

Judah Wright.

Also three Frenchmen who had lived in Deerfield some time, and who came from Canada.

Names of those who were slain at the Taking of the Town.

David Alexander.

Thomas Carter.

John Catlin.

Jonathan Catlin.

Sarah Field.

Samson Frary.

John French.

Alice Hawks.

John Hawks, jr., and his wife.
Thankful Hawks.
John Hawks.
Martha Hawks.
Samuel Hinsdale.
Joseph Ingersol.
Jonathan Kellogg.
Philip Mattoon's wife and child.
Parthena, (a negro.)
Henry Nims.*
Mary Nims.*
Mehitable Nims.*

Sarah Price.
Mary Root.
Thomas Shelden.
Mercy Shelden.
Samuel Smead's wife and two children.
Elizabeth Smead.
Martin Smith.
Serg. Benoni Stebbins.
Andrew Stevens.
Mary Wells.
John Williams, jr.
Jerusha Williams.

Slain in the Meadow.

Samuel Allis.
Serg. Boltwood.
Robert Boltwood.
Joseph Catlin.
Samuel Foot.

David Hoit, jr.
Jonathan Ingram.
Serg. Benjamin Wait.
Nathaniel Warner.

---

* These three were supposed to have been burned to death in a cellar.

JOURNAL OF REV. STEPHEN WILLIAMS.

THROUGH the politeness of Mrs. Jerusha M. Colton, formerly Miss Williams, of Longmeadow, a descendant of the Rev. John Williams, and granddaughter of the Rev. Dr. Stephen Williams, late of Springfield, I am indebted for the following Journal of her grandfather, kept during his captivity, and for other interesting matter relating to the early Indian war in this town and vicinity, written by him. It will be recollected that the Rev. Doctor Stephen Williams was a son of Mr. John Williams, and was taken prisoner with him at the last destruction of the town, at the age of eleven years. The following is his Journal, from his own handwriting : —

What befell Stephen Williams in his Captivity.

On the last of February, 1703–4, the French and Indians came and surprised our fort and took it, and after they had broken into our house and took us prisoners, they barbarously murdered a brother and sister of mine, as they did several of our neighbors. They rifled our house and then marched away with us that were captives, and set our house and barn on fire, as they did the greatest part of the town. When the greatest part of the enemy were gone out of the town, there came some English from the next town that drove those Indians that remained in the town away, but they were quickly driven back again by the rest of the army. Nine of them were slain as they retreated. Then they marched a little further and stopped, for they had several wounded men that hindered them. There they told us that, if the English pursued, they would kill us, otherwise they would not; but they quickly proved themselves liars, for before they departed from the place they barbarously murdered a child of about two years old. There my master took away my English shoes, and gave me Indian ones in the room of them, which I think were better to travel in. Then we marched five or six miles farther, where we took up our lodgings. Then one Englishman ran back to Deerfield, which provoked them much. They told us, that if any more ran away, they would burn the rest. There they slew our negro man. The next morning we travelled about two or three miles, when they murdered my ever honored mother, who having gone over a small river, which water running very swift flung her down, she, being wet, was not able to travel any farther. We travelled eight or nine miles farther and lodged that night. There some were disturbed, for some had five or six captives, and others none. They then called the captives together to make a more equal distribution, but I remained with my former master. Here they searched me and took away my silver buttons and buckles which I had on my shirt. Before we came to a small river, named West River, about thirty miles above Deerfield, they murdered three or four persons; where they had sleighs and dogs with which they drew their wounded men. They travelled (we thought) as if they designed to kill us all, for they travelled thirty-five or forty miles a day.

Here they killed near a dozen women and children, for their manner was, if any loitered, to kill them. My feet were very sore, so that I was afraid they would kill me also. We rested on the Sabbath day; they gave my father liberty to preach. Here we sang a psalm, for they requested of us a song. The next day we travelled a great way farther than we had at any time before. About the middle of the day, some that were in the rear fired at some geese that flew over, which put them into considerable fright, for they thought that the English were come up with them. Then they began to bind the prisoners, and to prepare themselves for battle, but when they understood what was the matter, they shot a volley for joy, boasting that the English could not overtake them.

I coming to my honored father, he told me he was taken lame in his ankle, which he sprained in the fall of the year. He said, likewise, he thought he should be killed, and if I should live to get to Canada, to tell them who I was, &c.; which then did terrify me much; but it pleased the Lord to strengthen him to perform his journey.

The next day was tempestuous, and I froze one of my feet; the day after, which was Wednesday, my master bid me go down to the river with him very early in the morning, which startled me, for he did not use to be so early. There that river parted, and I went up one branch, and my father with my brother and sisters another. I never saw my father for fourteen months. I did not eat any thing in the morning, yet must travel all day, yea, I travelled till about nine o'clock at night without one morsel of victuals. I travelled about fifty miles that day and night. For my supper I had one spoonful of Indian corn, in the morning five or six kernels, but must travel. Then we left the river and travelled about noon on the west side of the river. We came to two wig-wams, where we found the signs of Indians, but no Indians. (In those wigwams they left their sacks and went a hunting, if perhaps they might find some moose buried in the snow by the hunting Indians, but could not find any.)

I wandered about and lost myself, and hollowed. My master came to me, and was very angry. He lifted up the breach of his gun in order to kill me, but God kept back his hand, for which I desire his name might be praised. The Indians will never allow any body to hollow in the woods. Their manner is to make a noise like wolves, or other wild creatures, when they would call to one another. My master sent the Indian lad and I to those wigwams, but he himself took his gun and went a hunting (now there were only we three in company, we had left all that army). We made a fire, but had no victuals to dress, only a moose's paunch and bones, which the Indians had left. There we tarried that night, and the next day till about noon; then there came an

Indian girl and brought us some moose's meat dried, which I thought was the best victuals ever I ate. We travelled with the Indian girl about ten miles, where were two wigwams. My master that left us the day before was there. While we tarried here, the French that were in the army passed by. Within a day or two we travelled seven or eight miles northward, to a place where they had killed some moose, where they made wigwams (for their manner was when they killed any moose to move to them and lie by them till they had eaten them up). Now there were two Englishmen of our town in company with me, who came from the army, to wit, Deacon Hoit, and one Jacob Hix, a soldier (now my master was not yet come to his own family). From hence he went to look for his family, and within a day or two sent for me. I thought this was hard to go away alone. Here I left Deacon Hoit and Jacob Hix. Deacon Hoit I never saw more, for he was dead before I came from hunting. I went with the messenger, and after a tedious day's travel came to my master's family. He gave me to his brother, with whom I continued two or three months thereabouts, hunting moose, bears, and beavers. But when I first arrived here they were extraordinary kind, took care of my toe which was frozen, would not suffer me to do any work, gave me deer-skin to lie on, and a bear-skin to cover me withal; but this did not last long, for I was forced to carry such a pack when I travelled that I could not rise up without some help, was forced to cut wood, and carry it sometimes a considerable way on my back. After that manner I lived till their hunting time was over, without any society but the inhuman pagans.

We travelled with the design to go to Cowass, where was their rendezvous; but before we had got quite there, we met some Indians that stopped us. They told us that all the Indians were coming away from Cowass, which within a day or two came to be true. Now the reason of their deserting that place was this: there came an Englishman with six of

taken. The French were kind to me, gave me bread, which I had not eaten in a great while. They told me my father and brothers and sisters were got to Canada, which I was glad to hear of, for I was afraid my youngest brother was killed.

While I tarried here, a Frenchman came and desired the Indians to let me go with him, which they did. He gave me some victuals, and made me lie down in his couch, which my master's son perceiving, told his father, who thought he did it to hide me, and did design to steal me; upon which he came up and fetched me away, and would not let me go to the fort any more, for which I suffered. While here the French dressed my feet that were wounded, at which the Indians seemed to be vexed.

From hence we went towards Sorel, but tarried a day or two near a Frenchman's house, about three miles from Shamblee, who was kind to me, and would have lodged me in his house, but the Indians would not allow of it, mistrusting he would convey me away in the night privately. From hence we went to Sorel, and as soon as we had landed, there came a woman across the river on purpose to bring me some victuals, and seemed to pity me.

Here we tarried a day or two. My master bid me go to the fort a visiting, which was about fourscore rods off. I went, and at a Frenchman's persuasion tarried all night, and till next day about noon, when my master came for me; he was very angry with me, and after that would never suffer me to go to a French house alone. From this place we went to St. Francis, the Indian fort. My master could not comply with their rites and customs, whereupon he went to Albany and gave me to his kinsman, Sagamore George. But while I remained there, Monsieur Shamblee heard that I was with Sagamore George, and came to buy me. I seemed to be willing to go with him, at which the Indians were much disturbed, and would not let me go, because I showed a forwardness to go, and did likewise threaten to kill me, did complain to the Jesuit, who came and said to me, "What, no love Indian! they have saved your life," &c.

It is no wonder that the children will not speak to their friends when they come to see them, but they will scoff at and deride them, because the Indians have so taught them, and will be angry if they do otherwise.

While I lived here, I observed that some English children would scoff at me, and when before the Indians, worse than the Indian children, but when alone they would talk familiarly with me in English, about their own country, &c., whereas when before the Indians they would pretend that they could not speak English. Here the Indians did say something to me about religion, but not much ; being Eastern Indians, were not zealous as the Macquas are.

The French Governor, after he heard I was in the country, because of my father's entreaties, was often sending to the Indians to buy me, who were quite wearied out because of the many messages he sent. The Governor was not willing to give above thirty crowns, whereas they stood for forty. At length, being wearied out, my master went to the Jesuit, and got pen, ink, and paper, would have me write to my father, for we had heard he was learned, and had two hundred pounds a year allowed him, which I believe some of them believed. After he had got paper he takes another Indian with him that could speak good English, who was to indite for me. The substance of the letter was this, that if they did not buy me before spring, they would not sell me afterwards, and that he must give forty crowns for me. They carried it to the Jesuit, who could speak English, to see whether I had written as they ordered me, and when they found I had, they were well pleased.

My master had a mind to go hunting, and would have taken me with him ; but because he sent such word, that they must buy by such a time, he left me at home, that I might be ready if they should send to buy me, and when Captain Livingston and Mr. Sheldon were come to Canada, my mistress thought there would be an exchange of prisoners, and lest the French should then take me away for nothing, she removed up into the woods, about half a mile from the river, that if they came they might not find me. While on a certain day my mistress went to a French house to get victuals, and ordered me to spend my day in getting wood; but it proved a tempestuous day, and we had half a cart-load at the door, which is a great deal for Indians to have, so that I did not get any. When she came home, being disturbed by the French, asked what I had been doing; they replied, nothing, at which she was very angry. I will not beat you myself, says she, for my husband ordered me to the contrary, but will tell the Jesuit, the next time he comes. Within a day or two the Jesuit came. She was as good as her word, and did complain. He took me out and whipt me with a whip with six cords, several knots in each cord.

After a few days he came again, with a letter from my father, by which I understood he was a prisoner. I told the Indians, who said they believed it. He likewise said in his letter that the Governor of New England would take care we should be redeemed.

Whilst I lived here, I made about fourscore weight of sugar with the sap of maple trees, for the Indians. My mistress had a mind to go to Sorel, and because there was a barrel of sap to boil she sent me to the sugar place over night to boil it, so that we might go in the morning. I went and kept a good fire under the kettle, little thinking of its coming to sugar, and it was spoiled for want of stirring, for the manner is to stir it when it comes almost to sugar. They were very angry, and would not give me any victuals.

It being now spring, we went in canoes to Sorel; and so soon as we had got there, the woman that brought me victuals across the river when I was there before, came and desired of the Indians to let me go to the fort, which they consented to. I went; but remembering the bad effect of tarrying all night before, durst not do so again without the Indians' leave. I went to the Indians and carried them some victuals, and asked them to let me lie at the fort, which they granted. I kept here about a fortnight, and lay at the fort every night.

When we came to St. Francis we went to master's land, where I made preparation to plant corn; but before we began, the Governor came and bought me, after a long parley, for forty crowns. With him I went to Sorel, where I met with Captain Livingston and several captives. Captain Livingston told me I should go home to New England with him, which revived me much; — but the Governor quickly altered his mind, and said I must not go from hence.

I went down to Quebec with the Lord Intendant. When I arrived I found several English people that were prisoners. Here one Mr. Hill took care of me, and cut my hair for me (now my hair was like an Indian's, one side long and the other short). He got me a shirt, and a pair of breeches, and a jacket and stockings.

From hence, on the 11th of May, I was sent to live with my father at Chateauviche. While here, the French were very courteous and kind to me, as they were to my father. This seemed almost home to me, because my father I had not seen for fourteen months. When Mr. Dudley came to Canada, my father and I were sent to Quebec. When we were at Quebec, Captain Courtamouch took us to his house and entertained us very nobly. He said he had received kindness at New England. While we were at Quebec, the Seminary, a famous building, was burnt. And upon Mr. Dudley and Captain Vetch petitioning, the Governor gave me liberty to come home; and accordingly I came home on the 12th of October, 1705, but I left my honored father and brothers and sisters behind; and, after a tedious voyage, I arrived safe at Boston, in New England, on the 21st of November, 1705. And I desire that the name of God may be praised and adored for his wonderful goodness to me in sparing my life when I was as it were on the brink of eternity, and that he stayed the hands of those that took up their weapons to y me with them.

N. B. That while with the Indians I was in great danger of being drowned several times.

Extract from Rev. Dr. Stephen Williams's Journal.

September 16, 1696. John Smead and John Gillet, being in the woods hunting bees, were beset by a company of French Mohawks. Gillet was taken prisoner, and Smead escaped. The Indians fearing a discovery by Smead, sixteen of them hastened away towards the town, and three were left with Gillet. It being lecture-day, the people were got out of the meadows that they might attend the lecture, so that the enemy came as far as Mr. Daniel Belding's house,* within gunshot of the fort. Mr. Belding, being belated about his work, had but just got home from the field, and left his cart that was loaded with corn, and went into the house; and the Indians rushed upon them, and took him prisoner and his son Nathaniel, aged twenty-two years, and daughter Esther, aged thirteen years, and killed his wife and his son Daniel, and John, and his daughter Thankful. They took his son Samuel from the cart, but he kicked and scratched and bit so, that the Indian set him down and struck the edge of his hatchet into the pate of his head, and then pulled out his hatchet and left him for dead. His brains followed the hatchet; but he revived, and got to the fort, where there was care taken of him, and, notwithstanding the wound that he had, it pleased God and his life was spared; his wound healed, and he is yet living. He was once or twice accounted to be dead, and once accounted as dead a day or two after his being wounded. Abigail Belding, another daughter, was shot in the arm as she was running to the fort, but it was generally thought the bullet that struck her came from the fort. Sarah Belding, another of the daughters, hid herself amongst some tobacco in the chamber, and so escaped. The people in the fort, being then at the public worship, were alarmed, shot from the fort, and wounded one of the enemy in the fleshy part of the thigh.

---

* On the ground where Mr. Ralph Williams now lives.

The Indians fired at the fort, and wounded one Mr. Williams as he went out of the gate.

The enemy presently withdrew, (they were not one quarter of an hour in doing the exploit,) and were followed by some brisk young men into the meadow, who came within thirty rods and fired at them, and the Indians at them again, without damage on either side. The Indians killed some cattle that were feeding in the meadows. A boy that had the care of the cattle hid himself in the weeds, and escaped. The enemy went up the Green River and came to the companions they had left with Gillet. John Smead came into the house soon after Mr. Belding's family were well off. The first night the enemy lodged in a round hole near the river above the rock in New Hampshire, and from thence pursued their way to Canada by the way of Otter Creek, leaving Connecticut River, &c. When they came near Otter Creek, they came upon some tracks of Albany Indians that were going to Canada ; — for in those times the Indians from Albany were wont to go a scalping, as they call it, to Canada. They sent out their scouts and were upon the look-out, and at length discovered their smoke. And then they flung down their packs and painted themselves, and tied their English captives to trees and left two men to guard them, and proceeded on their business. Having divided themselves into two companies, they fell upon the savage company, which consisted of six men, and killed two of them, wounded two, and two escaped. Among the slain was one Uroew, an Indian known among the English, and supposed to be a bloody fellow. Of their own men, one was wounded near the fleshy part of the thigh, as one had before been at Deerfield. The prisoners were one a Schaghticook Indian, and the other a young Albany Mohawk. When the skirmish was over, the English were brought up, and so they proceeded on their journey. Mr. Belding asked the Schaghticook Indian (now his fellow-prisoner) what the enemy would do with them, who replied, that they would not kill the English prisoners, but give some of them to the French, and keep some of them themselves; but he expected to be burnt himself; but when they came to the lake, one rainy night, they made no fires, and some of them lodged under the canoes, from which this Schaghticook made his escape, having loosed himself by some means from his cords, &c.; and although he was pursued, the enemy could not recover him. As for the young Albany Mohawk, he was kept alive, being one of their own nation. The French Mohawk went, on their return to Canada, to the sect of the Romish religion. When Mr. Belding and company came to the fort called Oso, the males were obliged to run the gantlet. Mr. Belding, being a very nimble and light-footed man, received but few blows, save at first setting out, but the other two men were much abused by clubs, fire-brands, &c.

They arrived at Canada; and now they found what the Schaghticook Indian said to be true, for the Indians kept Mr. Belding himself and his daughter with them, and gave John Gillet and Nathaniel Belding to the French. Gillet worked as a servant to the nuns at their farm, and Nathaniel Belding worked for the Holy Sisters.

On the night of the 9th of July following, Mr. Belding was sold to the French, and lived as a servant with the Jesuits at the Seminary. His business was to wait upon them, and cut wood, make fires, &c., and tend the garden, and account-ed himself favorably dealt by, &c. In the winter following, Colonel Abraham Schuyler, with some others, came to Can-ada, and brought with them a copy of the articles of peace between England and France, and returned home with some Dutch captives.

In April following, Colonel Peter Schuyler, and Colo-ne A. Schuyler, and the Dutch Domine, with some others, came to Canada, and the French Governor gave liberty to all captives, English and Dutch, to return home; — yea, allowed them to obligate under sixteen years of age to return with them; those above that age were to be at their liberty, &c.

These Dutch gentlemen gathered up all the captives, both
English and Dutch, that they could find, and returned June
8; took Mr. Belding and his children, and Martin Smith,
with about twenty more English, with them, and arrived at
Albany in about fifteen days, where the Dutch people treated
him with a great deal of kindness, and offered to send him
home directly to Deerfield. Colonel Schuyler clothed him
and his children, at the desire of his brother, Mr. John Bel-
ding, of New York, who paid him for the clothes, &c. After
about three weeks' stay at Albany, Mr. Belding and his chil-
dren went down the river to New York, where his brother
had provided a place for his entertainment. From York he
went in a vessel to Stamford, and from thence returned to
New York, and after some stay there, returned to Deerfield.
John Gillet got home a little before him by the way of France,
and so to England, having received great kindness in England.

An Account of some Ancient Things. From the same.

Capt. Wright, Lieut. Wells, —— Wright, Jabez Olm-
stead, Job Strong, Jonathan Hoit, Tim. Childs, John Burt,
and Tim. Pagan, and Joshp Ephn., at the lake went with-
in four miles of Shamblee, killed one and wounded three,
and at French River killed eight. Leaving B. and Lieut.
Wells, and John S. wounded. They got one canoe with
their prisoners. This was next day after the expedition at
the lake; slept at White River Eli Severance, Thomas Mc-
Crary, Joseph Root, and Sergeant Wait.

Deerfield, May 10, 1704. John Allen and his wife, going
out from the garrison about two miles upon some business,
were ambushed by the Indians, who killed him outright, and
took his wife, whom they killed about a mile or two from the
place.

About the middle of July, 1704, a friend Indian was killed

at Hatfield Mill; his name was Kindniss. The enemy had not time to scalp him.

On the same week, Thomas Russel, a young man of Hatfield, being then a soldier of Deerfield, was sent out into the woods with men as a scout, but he, rambling from his company, was killed by the Indians.

Some time in May or June, 1705, Joseph Petty, John Nims, Thomas Baker, and Martin Kellogg, jr. made their escape from Montreal, and got home to Deerfield, &c.

July 13, 1704. One Dr. Crossman, with two or three more men, were riding in the night between Hadley and Springfield, and were fired upon by the enemy, who wounded Dr. Crossman in the arm. This is the only time that I can learn that they ever fired upon any body in the night.

July 31, 1706. Samuel Chapin and his brother went up to their farm, perceiving signs of Indians, at a place called Chicopee, in the north part of Springfield. They hastened toward the town, but the Indians followed them about a mile and a half, and then fired upon them, and shot Samuel Chapin through the side, but he recovered of his wound. The same company of Indians, as it is supposed, went to Brookfield, and killed the widow Taft as she was milking.

July 9, 1708. Samuel and Joseph Parsons, of Northampton, sons to Captain John Parsons, being in the woods looking after cattle, were slain by the Indians.

July 26, 1708. About seven or eight Indians rushed into the house of Lieutenant Wright, at a place called Skipmuck, in Springfield, and killed and scalped, and they beat their heads to pieces, Aaron Parsons, and Barijah Hubbard, who were soldiers; knocked down and scalped old Mr. Wright, who yet lived about three months and then died; two children of Henry Wright, that lay in the cradle, they knocked on the head; one of them died that night, the other recovered, and is still living. They took Henry Wright's wife captive, whom it is supposed they afterwards killed and scalped. Lieutenant Wright got out of his shop window, and made his escape ; and a daughter of his ran out at a door which latched on the outside, and pulled the string after her, and so escaped. The house was not fortified, but had flankers at two corners, &c.

October 30, 1708. Abijah Bartlet was killed at Brookfield, and Joseph Jennings and Benjamin Jennings and John Green were wounded ; a boy of John Woolcot's was taken.

October 26, 1708. Ebenezer Field, of Hatfield, going to Deerfield, was killed near Muddy, or, as some call it, Bloody Brook, for there it was that Captain Lathrop and his company were cut off in Philip's war.

August, 1708. A scout of six men, about an hundred miles above Deerfield, were fell upon by a party of Indians, and one Robert Windsor was slain ; but after he had received his mortal wound, he got upon his knees and shot the very Indian that shot him, and fell down and died. So that when the Indians came to them, which was within a few minutes, they were both dead, lying within a few rods one of another. This account I had of an Indian, who, upon relating the matter, added, " No, he is not Barber, but his ghost." At the same time Martin Kellog was taken, which was the second time of his going into captivity, but before he was taken, discharged his gun and wounded an Indian in his thigh.

April 11, 1709. Mr. Mehuman Hinsdale was driving his team from Northampton, without any fear of Indians (the leaves not being put forth) ; was met by two Indians about half a mile from the Pine Bridge in Hatfield North Meadow, who took him prisoner, and carried him away into the West Woods. The Indians were civil and courteous to him on their journey. They arrived at Shamblee within about eleven days and a half. After they took Mr. Hinsdale from Shamblee, they carried him to Oso, the fort, where he was obliged to run the gantlet, as they call it, for near three quarters of a mile, but he ran so swiftly as not to receive a blow till he came near the fort, when he was met by an Indian, who, taking hold of the line that was round his neck, and hung upon his back, pulled him down, and so he was struck by one fellow. After he was got into the fort, he was set in the midst of the company, and obliged to sing and dance, and while thus employed, he was struck a very severe blow upon his naked back by a youth of such an age as to think of engaging in some warlike expedition; but this, being contrary to their usual custom, (he having performed the ceremony of running the gantlet,) was resented, not only by Mr. Hinsdale, the sufferer, but by the Indians in general. From this fort Mr. Hinsdale was carried to the French Governor, who knew him (for this was the second time of Mr. Hinsdale's captivity), and told him he expected a full account of what news, especially about an expedition which he suspected was on foot. The Governor told him if he would give him a full account of what there was in his country, he would treat him with respect; but if he found he did not, he would use him worse than a *Devil*, &c. But Mr. Hinsdale avoided what he could toward giving him an account ; but when Mr. Whitney of Billerica was brought into the country by the Indians, and gave an account of an expedition on foot, Mr. Hinsdale was taken and put into the dungeon, &c.

After a while the Indians desired of the Governor that they might have Mr. Hinsdale to burn, pretending they would fight the better against the English if they could burn an Englishman, and he was delivered to the Indians, who were plotting to leave the French and go over to General Nicholson and the Dutch, and designed to make use of Mr. Hinsdale to have introduced them, &c. He was recaptivated from the French, and Mr. Hinsdale was led away towards Montreal from Quebec. The Indians communicated their design to Mr. Hinsdale, who was overjoyed with the account (for he thought of nothing but being sacrificed by them), and encouraged it ; but before they were ready to execute their design, a certain Indian fell sick, and in his sickness making confession to a priest, discovered the plot, and so all was dashed.

The fellow that was the projector of it (being one that had come from Albany upon some of the Five Nations and to them) had timely notice to escape to Shamblee, where he put a trick upon the officer of the fort, pretending to him that he was sent by the Governor to make what discovery if the English supplied him with arms, ammunition, and provisions; and he had been gone but a little while into the wood before his pursuers (the plot being wholly ripped up) came after him; but he was gone, so as to escape his pursuers. Mr. Hinsdale was taken from the Indians, and again committed to prison, and the next year Mr. Hinsdale and Mr. Joseph Clesson were sent to France in a man-of-war; and in France he met with great kindness, particularly from the Lord Intendant of Rochelle, and after a while they were shipped at St. Melores for London, where they met with great kindness, especially from Mr. Agent Dummer, who interceded with the Lords of the Admiralty, who ordered them on board one of the Queen's ships, which brought them to Rhode Island, from whence they got home in safety, after Mr. Hinsdale had been absent from his family about three years and a half.

[About the 1st of June, 1836, I copied the inscription on the old tomb-stone of Mehuman Hinsdale, in our old burying-yard. It is on a beautiful light-blue slate-stone, one of the most durable kinds of stone for monuments, and, in my opinion, far superior to marble. The grave-stone of the second wife of the Rev. John Williams is of the same material, and one of the finest in this yard.

"Here lies buried the body of Lievt. Mehuman Hinsdell, died May y⁰ 9, 1736, in the 63d year of his age, who was the first male child born in this place, and was twice captivated by the Indian Salvages.

"Math. 5th – 7th — 'Blessed are the merciful, for they shall obtain mercy.' "]

August, 1709.   John Clary and Robert Granger were slain at Brookfield.

July 22, 1710.   John Grosvenor, Ebenezer Howard, John

White, Benjamin and Stephen Jennings, and Joseph Kellogg, were slain in the meadow at Brookfield.

August 10, 1711. Samuel Strong of Northampton, with his son Samuel, going in the morning very early into the field, were ambuscaded by a party of Indians, who fired upon them and killed and scalped the young man, and wounded the old gentleman in the shoulder, and then took him captive and carried him to Canada ; but he has since returned home again.

July 29, 1712. Benjamin Wright, a lad, son to Joseph Wright of Skipmuck, in Springfield, being in a meadow at Skipmuck, was taken by the Indians, and afterwards killed in the woods, as was supposed.

July 30, 1712. A scout of men that was out above Deerfield, being very careless and noisy as they travelled, were fired upon by a party of Indians, who killed Samuel Andross, and took Jonathan Barrett and William Sanford captives.

June 18, 1724. A small company of Indians fell upon some men in Hatfield, at a place called the Mill Swamp, about four miles from town, and killed Benjamin Smith, and took captive Joseph Allis and Aaron Wells. The men they killed within a day or two, &c.

July 10, 1724. Timothy Childs and Samuel Allen were wounded by the Indians in Deerfield Meadow ; but they recovered of their wounds, &c.

THE BARRS FIGHT.

In order to render the history of Indian battles, which are necessarily connected with the biography of Mr. Williams, complete, it is thought advisable to give some account of the Barrs Fight, so called, as this was the last incursion of the Indians against the town of Deerfield.

In the year 1744, the war again commenced between France and Great Britain, and the Indians again became the allies of France. From 1725 to 1745 there were scarcely any Indian depredations in Deerfield or its vicinity. In 1745 there were several skirmishes with the Indians in various parts of the country, but none within the borders of Deerfield, or in which her citizens were engaged.

On the 25th of August, 1746, occurred the Barrs Fight, at the southwest part of Deerfield Meadows. The following relation was given me by Miss Eunice Allen, who on that day was tomahawked by an Indian, but survived the cruel wound. Miss Allen was above eighty years of age when she gave me the history. She had at this time been confined to her bed more than sixteen years, but her recollection was very clear and distinct. She remembered the events of that day as perfectly as if they had taken place yesterday. Her account agrees with that of the Rev. Mr. Taylor, published in 1793.

Fort Massachusetts, at the western foot of Hoosac Mountain, about thirty miles west of Deerfield, was taken on the 20th of August, 1746. After the capitulation, a party of Indians, meditating an attack upon Deerfield, came down upon the borders of the meadows, and reconnoitred them. They first examined the North Meadow, and then the South. Finding a quantity of hay in the South Meadow, two miles south of the Street, and supposing that our people would be there at work the next day, they concealed themselves in the brush and underwood upon the borders of the adjoining hills. The next day, ten or twelve men and children, the men armed with guns, which they always carried with them, went into the field and commenced their labor. A Mr. Eleazer Hawks was out hunting partridges on the hills, where the Indians lay, that morning. He saw a partridge, and shot it. This alarmed the Indians, who supposed they were discovered. They immediately killed and scalped Mr. Hawks, and then proceeded to attack the workmen. They fought some time, which gave some of the children an opportunity to escape. Mr. Allen, father of Miss Allen, resolutely maintained his ground in defence of three children, who were at work with him in the field, until he killed one or two of the enemy. When he was overpowered, he fought them with the breech of his gun, but he was finally shot, and horribly mangled. The shirt which he wore on that day, torn with many balls and gashed with tomahawks, is still to be seen, as a curiosity, either in the Museum in Deerfield Academy, or at the house of his grandson, at the Barrs. In this engagement three men and a boy were killed, one boy was taken prisoner, and Miss Allen was wounded in the head, and left for dead, but not scalped. In endeavoring to make her escape, she was pursued by an Indian with an uplifted tomahawk and a gun. She was extremely active, and would have outrun him, had he not fired upon her. The ball missed her, but she supposed that it had struck her, and in her fright she fell. The Indian overtook her, and buried his tomahawk in her head, and left her for dead. The firing in the meadows alarmed the people in the Street, who ran to the scene of action, and the Indians made a hasty retreat, and were pursued for several miles by a body of men under the command of Captain Clesson. Miss Allen was passed by a number of people, who supposed her to be dead. At last an uncle came to her, discovered signs of life, and conveyed her home. Her wound was dressed by Dr. Thomas Williams, who took from it considerable quantities of brain.

Samuel Allen, Jr., the boy who was taken in this engagement, was carried to Canada, and remained with the Indians a year and nine months. He was finally redeemed by Colonel John Hawks, of this town, who was a celebrated partisan officer in Indian warfare, and a most useful and worthy man, whose biography should be transmitted to posterity. He was extremely loth to see Colonel Hawks, who was his uncle, and when he came into his presence he refused to speak the English language, pretending to have forgotten it; and although he was dressed most shabbily, fared most miserably, and was covered with vermin, he was very much opposed to leaving the Indians. Threats and force were finally employed to make him consent to quit them, and he asserted to the day of his death, that the Indian mode of life was the happiest.

To give a complete view of all the Indian skirmishes which have ever occurred in the valley of the Connecticut, north of Springfield in Massachusetts, I shall subjoin the date of all those I have not heretofore enumerated. In July, 1745, the Indians attacked Great Meadow, above Fort Dummer on the Connecticut, and captivated William Phips; after marching half a mile, Phips killed one of his captors, and knocked down another, when he attempted to escape, but three of the enemy overtook and killed him. Josiah Fisher was killed and scalped about the same time, near Upper Ashuelot.

On the 11th of October, the Indians again attacked the fort at Great Meadow, but unsuccessfully. Nehemiah How was taken and carried to Quebec, where he died. On their return, they killed a man by the name of David Rugg. In April, 1746, the enemy took from No. 4 (Charlestown, New Hampshire), then the most northerly settlement on the Connecticut, Captain John Spafford, Isaac Parker, and Stephen Farnsworth, and carried them to Canada, and soon after, near Northfield, they killed Joshua Holton. On the 23d of this month a large party of Indians made an unsuccessful attempt upon the fort at the Upper Ashuelot. John Bullard and the wife of Daniel McKinne were killed, aud Nathan Blake was made prisoner.

Early in May, No. 4 was again attacked. Seth Putnam was killed. They were driven off by the intrepidity of Colonel Willard, having lost two of their number.

May 6th, an unsuccessful attack was made upon the fort at Fall-town (now Bernardstown). John Burke was wounded, though not severely. They burnt one house, and killed about ten cattle. The Indians lost two men. On that very day Sergeant John Hawks and John Miles were wounded by the Indians near Fort Massachusetts. Miles escaped to the fort. Hawks fought them for some time single-handed, and might have taken them both had he understood their language. They begged for quarter just before he turned to escape.

On the 10th of the same month, Matthew Clark with his wife and daughter at Colerain, were fired upon by five Indians who had been a short time before at Fall-town. Clark was killed outright, and his wife and daughter wounded. One of the Indians was killed by a soldier in the fort at Colerain, the rest retreated, and the wounded were brought in. Soon after, the enemy again attacked No. 4. Captain Stevens repulsed them with the loss of three men, viz. Aaron Lyon, Peter Perrin, and Joseph Marcy. Four of his men were wounded, and one taken captive.

On the 11th of June the Indians attacked Fort Massachusetts and were repulsed. They wounded Gershom Hawks and Elisha Nims, and captured Benjamin Tenter. The Indians lost one man.

No. 4 was again attacked on the 19th, and a gallant action maintained by Captains Stevens and Brown. The enemy were again driven back. Jedediah Winchel was killed, and David Parker, Jonathan Stanhope, and Noah Heaton were wounded, but recovered.

On the 20th, about twenty Indians attacked Bridgman's Fort, just below Fort Dummer. William Robbins and James Parker were killed; John Beaumont and Daniel How were captivated ; Michael Gilson and Patrick Ray were wounded, but recovered.

July 28th, the Indians took David Morrison, of Colerain, a prisoner.

August 3d, No. 4 was again attacked, and Ebenezer Phillips was killed. After this they retreated, after having burnt several buildings and killed many cattle and horses.

On the 11th, Benjamin Wright of Northfield was killed, while riding in the woods, by a shot from an Indian. Ezekiel Wallingford of Paquaig (now Athol), was killed and scalped on the 17th ; and on the same day a man by the name of Bliss was killed and scalped near Colerain or Bernardston on the road from Deerfield.

1747. Again No. 4 was unsuccessfully attacked. Two men by the names of Joseph Ely and John Brown were slightly wounded on the 7th of April.

Asahel Burt and Nathaniel Dickinson of Northfield were killed and scalped on the 15th. As the enemy returned from Northfield, they burnt the principal part of the buildings in Winchester and Lower Ashuelot, the inhabitants having previously deserted them.

On the 15th of July, Mr. Eliakim Sheldon of Bernardston was killed by an Indian, and some time in the course of this month John Mills of Colerain was also killed.

August 26th, the enemy appeared at Northampton, and killed and scalped Elijah Clark. John Smead was also killed and scalped, as he was travelling from Northfield to Sunderland.

A skirmish took place on the 24th of October, between twelve men who were passing down the river from No. 4, and a body of Indians. The enemy killed and scalped Nathaniel Gould and Thomas Goodell. Oliver Avery was wounded, and John Henderson was captivated. The rest escaped.

1748. March 15th, twenty Indians attacked about eight of our men who were out a few rods from No. 4. Charles

Stevens was killed, one Androus was wounded, and Eleazer Priest was captivated.

On the 9th of May, Noah Bixley of Southampton was killed and scalped.

As Captain Melvin with eighteen men about this time was at the lake near Crown Point, he fired at two canoes containing Indians. When on his return, being on the West River, thirty or forty miles above Fort Dummer, he was attacked by surprise by the Indians, and his men were dispersed. Some of them rallied and returned the fire of the enemy, and killed one of them. Melvin lost six men. The rest returned at intervals. The names of the men who were killed were Joseph Petty, John Heywood, John Dod, Daniel Mann, and Isaac Taylor. It is supposed Samuel Severance was captivated.

As thirteen men were marching from Colonel Hinsdale's, on the 13th, to Fort Dummer, they were attacked by a large body of Indians. Joseph Richardson, Nathan French, and John Frost were killed instantaneously. Henry Stevens, Ben. Osgood, William Blanchard, Matthew Wiman, Joel Johnson, Moses Perkins, and William Bickford were captivated. Bickford probably died of his wounds.

As Captain Hobbs from No. 4 was marching, on the 28th of June, through the woods with forty men, about twelve miles northwest of Fort Dummer¡ he was attacked by a large body of Indians, who pursued him. With much coolness, judgment, and deliberation, he arranged his men in order, and fought the enemy four hours with great bravery, and dispersed them. Captain Hobbs lost three men, viz. Ebenezer Mitchel, Eli Scott, and Samuel Gunn. Three also were wounded.

On the 14th of July, a scout of seventeen men, while passing from Colonel Hinsdale's to Fort Dummer, were fired upon by 120 Indians. Two of the scout were killed at the onset, two were wounded, four escaped, and the rest were captivated. The Indians killed the wounded, after they had proceeded with them about a mile. On the 23d, the Indians killed a man in Northfield Street, by the name of Aaron Belding.

On the 2d of August, two hundred of the enemy were hovering round Fort Massachusetts, which was then under the command of Captain, since Colonel, Ephraim Williams. The Indians fired upon a scout from the fort, and Captain Williams with thirty men went out to meet them, but their numbers were so great that he thought it best to return. In this action one Abbot was killed, and Lieutenant Hawley and Ezekiel Wells wounded, but not dangerously. This was the last mischief done by the enemy till the year 1755, as peace occurred between France and England in 1748, and war did not again break out till 1756. Nevertheless, the Indians began their depredations again in 1755, in the summer of which year a number of them appeared at Stockbridge, and killed several men and cattle. In June they attacked a party of men who were at work in the meadow in the upper part of Charlemont. Several escaped, but Captain Rice and Phineas Arms were killed, and their bodies were horribly mangled. A boy by the name of Titus King was taken prisoner. In the same month the Indians attacked Bridgman's Fort at Hinsdale, and carried it. Fourteen persons were captivated. Caleb Howe was killed. The remainder escaped. About the same time the fort at Keene, under the command of Captain Sims, was attacked with great fury, by a large body of Indians. They were repulsed with fortitude. No lives were lost on the part of the English, but many cattle were killed, and houses burnt. One person who was out of the fort was taken. They soon after appeared at the same fort, and took a man by the name of Frizzle.

In July a large body of the enemy again attacked Fort Hinsdale, and killed two men, one named Alexander, and took one prisoner. Nearly at the same time they killed two men at Bellows's Fort; and somewhat farther up the river a man by the name of Pike was killed.

1756. June 17th. At Winchester this day Josiah Foster and his family were captivated, and on the same day at Fort Massachusetts the Indians killed Benjamin King and a man by the name of Meacham. In June also they killed Lieutenant Joseph Willard at No 4.

On the 25th of the same month, a large body of Indians attacked a body of our men, who were returning from the army at the lake. Eight men were killed, and five taken prisoners.

Captain Chapin, and two persons by the name of Chidester, were killed by the Indians on the 11th of July, at a place called West Hoosac.

In the year 1757 the enemy made his appearance at No. 4, and took five persons prisoners.

On the 20th of March, 1758, the enemy fired on and wounded John Morrison and John Henry of Colerain, near North River, a branch of Deerfield River. They burnt Captain Morrison's barn, and killed his cattle, the same day. On the 21st, the Indians again made their appearance at Colerain, and took Joseph McCown and his wife prisoners. They killed Mrs. McCown the next day, she being unable to travel.

After this period the people in this section of the country were not molested by the Indians.

11

EXTRACT FROM A SERMON,

*Preached at Mansfield, August 4, 1741, at a Time set apart
for Prayer for the Revival of Religion, and on Behalf of
Mrs. Eunice, the Daughter of the Rev. Mr. John Williams
(formerly Pastor of Deerfield), who was then on a Visit
there, from Canada, where she has been long in Captivity:
by Solomon Williams, A. M., Pastor of the First Church
in Lebanon.*

" You may well think I have all along had some special
eye to the uncommon occasion of prayer at this time, for that
person here present with us, who has been for a long time in
a miserable captivity, with a barbarous and heathen people,
now for more than thirty-eight years; yet among that people
bred up in Popish superstition, blindness, and bigotry, who,
by the providence of God, came last year, and now again
with her husband and two of her children, on a visit to her
friends in New England. Some of you know well, and I am
sure I do, how long she has been the subject of prayer.
What numberless prayers have been put up to God for her by
many holy souls now in heaven, as well as many who yet
remain on earth! How many groans and fervent prayers
can these ears witness to have uttered and breathed forth with
a sort of burning and unquenchable ardor from the pious and
holy soul of her dear father, now with God! I know not that
ever I heard him pray, after his own return from captivity,
without a remembrance of her; that God would return her to
His sanctuary, and the enjoyment of the Gospel light and
grace in that purity and simplicity in which it shines in our
land. But in this it seemed as if he never could be denied;
that God would not let her perish in Popish superstition and
ignorance; but, let her place be where it would, that he
would, as he easily could, find some way for deliverance from
those snares and thick-laid stratagems of the Devil to beguile

and ruin poor souls, and make her a monument of his glorious and almighty grace. And this he was wont to do with such expressions of faith in God, and holy fervors of his soul, as seemed to breathe himself and her into the arms of the covenant of grace. God did not give him leave to see the performance of his wishes and desires for her, but took them to satisfy him in God himself, and make him perfectly know that not a tittle of the covenant should ever fail ; and left her in the same state, to try the faith and call forth the prayers of his people still. We now see some dawnings towards her deliverance, and living hopes of it ; though all endeavors of men to persuade her here have been heretofore tried in vain. It has pleased God to incline her the last summer, and now again of her own accord, to make a visit to her friends ; and seems to encourage us to hope that He designs to answer the many prayers which have been put up for her, and, by the mighty power of his providence and grace, to give us one extraordinary conviction that he is a God hearing prayer."

The following extract of a letter to me from Mrs. Jerusha M. Colton, on the same subject, dated Longmeadow, May 26th, 1836, is highly interesting, and I have no doubt she will pardon me for the freedom I have taken in transcribing it : —

"I send you an old sermon, thinking the occasion of it might interest you, if you have never seen it. Here is another testimony of one personally acquainted with my great-grandfather, of his deep piety, and I think a remarkable expression of it.

"My aunt Eunice was indeed the object of great solicitude. I have heard my dear mother say of my grandfather, as it is here said of my father, that she never heard him pray without remembering her. She made her first visit here in

ELEAZER WILLIAMS, GRANDSON OF EUNICE WILLIAMS.

A STRANGE story is going the rounds of the public papers and magazines, purporting that Eleazer Williams, the part-breed Indian, a descendant from Eunice mentioned above, who was taken captive at the time of the destruction of the town of Deerfield by the French and Indians in 1703 – 4, is the Dauphin, son of Louis the Sixteenth, late king of France. I have been acquainted with Eleazer ever since he was a young man, and have never heard his origin or his parentage doubted until within the last four or five years, and never from him before the year 1849. I have no doubt of his regular descent from Eunice Williams ; and, notwithstanding all that has been said about his having no Indian appearance about him and no Indian blood in his veins, I think in many respects he resembles an Indian half-breed. Let others who have seen him judge for themselves. He showed me a scar upon his side, which he said was in consequence of a wound he received in the late war with Great Britain. He request-ed me to examine the scar for the purpose of determining whether I thought such a wound would be sufficient to entitle him to a pension from Congress. I do not know how much the color of his skin may have altered since then, under his dress, but at that time it was more the color of an Indian than a white man.

Although I have known him since he was quite young, yet I have never discovered any traces of idiocy about him, as alleged ; and others, who have known him when he was a boy, coincide with me in this opinion.

The astounding announcement which was said to have been made to him by De Joinville, at Green Bay, in 1841, that he was the Dauphin, son of Louis the Sixteenth, late king of France, seemed not to have obtained much notoriety till several years afterwards. This alleged conference may be found in Putnam's Magazine for February, 1853. Prince de Joinville was son of Louis Philippe, a relative of Louis the Sixteenth, who was beheaded in the French Revolution, and distant presumptive heir to the throne of France. If the Dauphin's title to the throne was extinguished, then one bar to De Joinville's accession to the throne would be removed, and to effect this was supposed to be the object of the Prince's visit to Eleazer.

If it was true that Eleazer believed himself to be the Dauphin, why was he so long silent upon the subject? Scarce a lisp of it reached my ears for nearly five years. In the year 1846 I prepared and wrote a "Genealogy and History of the Williams Family in America," which was published in a large-sized duodecimo volume, with plates, in the year 1847. As I had but little knowledge of Eleazer's family beyond his descent from Eunice Williams by her Indian husband, I requested him to give me an account of them, and in 1846 — five years after his conversation with De Joinville — he gave me the substance of the following notice of his family, without ever making the most distant allusion to his royal descent, or to his ever having had an interview with De Joinville. The reader can judge whether, if he believed himself to be of royal descent, he would not have alluded to the fact.

My book relates, that Eunice Williams, who was carried captive to Canada in the year 1704, when eight years of age, was daughter of the Rev. John Williams, first minister of Deerfield ; was born September 17, 1696, and died in captivity at the age of ninety years. At the time Mr. Williams was redeemed, she was left among the Indians, and no money could procure her redemption. She soon forgot the English language, became an Indian in her habits, married an Indian, who, it is said, assumed the name of Williams, though the Rev. Eleazer Williams of Green Bay states that his great-grandmother married an Indian by the name of De Rogers, and had three children, one son, John, and two daughters.

He says it is not true, as has been heretofore stated, that the
Indian who married Eunice assumed the name of Williams,
but that he (Eleazer) received the name of Williams legiti-
mately, or in course, as I shall mention subsequently. John,
the only son of Eunice, was killed in the French and Indian
wars under the celebrated partisan Rogers, at Rogers's Rock,
at Lake George, in 1758. Some years after her marriage,
Eunice visited Deerfield in her Indian dress. She attended
meeting in her father's church while here, and her friends
dressed her in the English fashion. She indignantly threw
off her clothes in the afternoon, and resumed the Indian
blanket. Every effort was made to persuade her to leave
the Indians and remain among her relations, but in vain.
She preferred the Indian mode of life and the haunts of the
Indians, to the unutterable grief of her father and friends.
Her descendants have frequently visited Deerfield since, and
claimed a relationship with the family and descendants of
the Rev. Mr. Williams, and been treated kindly by them.

I understand by Eleazer, that Charles B. Sallerville, a re-
lation, has written her biography in a large manuscript vol-
ume. According to Eleazer, her children by John De
Rogers were John, who died in infancy; Sarah, who mar-
ried a Williams; Catherine, who married Francis Ilere
Rice. Their child was Thomas, an only son and only de-
scendant from her. He married Marian De Rice, a daugh-
ter of one of the captives from Marlborough, Mass. Their
children were Catherine, died 1802, aged 24; Thomas, sup-
posed to be dead; William, died 1831; Eleazer; Louis;
John; Peter, died 1802; Mary Ann, Charles Pitkin, who
both died young; and Jarvis.

Sarah, daughter of Eunice above, who was captured at
Deerfield, married an English physician by the name of Wil-
liams in the year 1758. The story told me by Eleazer, her
grandson, in relation to this man, is substantially as follows:
— " In the French war of 1755 – 60, an English fleet was
sent out against the French, which separated in a tremendous

storm near the coast of Nova Scotia. Dr. Williams was on
board one of the vessels, which was afterwards taken by a
French man-of-war. As Dr. Williams was a man of sci-
ence and a distinguished physician, he was treated with a
great deal of attention by the French physicians in Canada.
He was a botanist, and was suffered to ramble in various
parts of Canada, and was carried by the Indians in their ca-
noes to several of their towns. At Caughnawaga he became
acquainted with Sarah, the daughter of Eunice, and married
her, on condition that he would not move from Canada. This
physician proved to be the son of the Bishop of Chichester in
England. They had one son, Thomas Williams, the father
of Eleazer Williams, whom I have seen at Deerfield when I
was a boy. He was a captain in the British service during
the American Revolutionary War. Thomas married a
Frenchwoman ; so that Eleazer, according to his own state-
ment, has part English, part Indian, and part French blood
in his veins. He had several sons; among the rest, Rev.
Eleazer Williams, of Green Bay, who was born not far from
the year 1790. He was educated in the United States, and
studied his profession, if I recollect right, with the celebrated
Dr. Moses Welch, of Mansfield, Conn. He is now (1847)
preaching to the remnant of the Stockbridge tribe of Indians
at Green Bay, in Wisconsin Territory. He is an Episco-
palian in Deacon's orders, though educated a Congregational-
ist. He has received marked attention throughout the coun-
try, and is a highly distinguished man. He married Miss
Mary Hobart Jourdan, a distant relative of the king of
France, from whom he has been honored with several splen-
did gifts, among the rest a golden cross and star. He has
one son, by the name of John.''

Nearly the whole of the above statements, as I have men-
tioned, I had from Eleazer himself, five years after his con-
ference with De Joinville. The public can attach what im-
portance to them they please.

In relation to his age, Eleazer has frequently told me that

he was born about the year 1790. By this he did not mean five years before, or five years after. We have often compared ages, and he has called his age about the same as mine, and I was born in the year 1790. Mr. Hale, Editor of the Boston Daily Advertiser, with whose father, at Westhampton, Eleazer lived for some time, says, when he first saw him, in 1800, he was then but ten years of age. The late Governor Williams, of Vermont, who was intimately acquainted with him, even from a youth, thinks he was born about the year 1790. While at my house in the year 1851, after having for the first time in my hearing talked over the subject of his being the Dauphin, some one of my family inquired of him concerning his age, and he replied, " If I am a Williams, I am so old ; but if I am the Dauphin, I am older." The Dauphin was born in 1785, consequently Eleazer is about five years younger, which must be fatal to his claims.

In relation to his conversation with De Joinville, he has frequently told me and my family that his visit from the Prince was in consequence of his relationship to his wife, and that he received his presents from the same cause. His stories here were much at variance with those in the Magazine.

It appears from letters which I have from time to time received from Eleazer, in addition to the genealogy mentioned above, that he persisted for a number of years after his alleged conversation with De Joinville in acknowledging his descent from the Rev. John Williams of Deerfield, whom he uniformly speaks of as his *grandsire*, although removed to the fourth generation from him. Nothing is more common than speaking of progenitors and relations in the fourth generation, and even further removed, as grandparents, uncles, &c.

He wrote me from Green Bay on the 27th of December, 1845, as follows : " I am highly pleased to learn that you are tracing out the genealogy of the Williams family, and particularly of my *grandfather*, Rev. John Williams."

In a letter to me from Green Bay, bearing date August

3d, 1846, after speaking of a discourse which he intended to prepare and deliver to the inhabitants of Deerfield, in relation to the life and character of the Rev. John Williams, first minister of Deerfield, he says : " I am still desirous to pay a tribute of respect to the memory of my departed *grandsire*. Although the materials in hand for a biography are some- what scanty, yet I am in hopes that I shall be able to collect sufficient, from the bureaus of the descendants in your State, to make the discourse interesting, particularly to our family."

He proposed a contribution for two discourses before the citizens of this town. He delivered them on two successive evenings, before very small audiences. I should hardly think there were thirty people at the last lecture. A contri- bution was taken up, and I think not much more than three dollars was raised. Mr. Williams went directly from Deer- field to Boston, and about that time there appeared an an- nouncement in one of the Boston papers, that his lectures had been received with great applause by very large and respect- able audiences at Deerfield. It is not an uncommon thing for two hundred and fifty people, and sometimes many more, to attend such lectures here.

Extract from a letter from him, dated Green Bay, October 21st, 1846 : —

" Dr. S. W. Williams : —

" Dear Sir, — As you have expressed a strong desire to know whether the portrait of my *grandsire* (Rev. John Wil- liams) can be obtained for the object you have in view, I have to say that it will afford me peculiar pleasure to aid you in your laudable undertaking by putting the same into your hands.

" I am, dear Sir, your affectionate kinsman,
" E. Williams."

In a letter to me of September 30th, 1847, dated at Buf- falo, he says : " In accordance to your request, I have this day sent you a portrait of my *grandfather Williams*, taken in daguerreotype. Although it is a correct or good representation, says one, yet it is rather too faint." I received this portrait too late to insert it in my genealogy of the Williams family, and returned it to him soon after.

Now, on the 4th of July, 1849, eight years after the astonishing communication of De Joinville that he was the lost Dauphin, the son of Louis the Sixteenth, and after the subject had been discussed in the public papers, he for the *first time* communicates to me doubts of his origin and descent. He says, in a letter of that date: " As to my pedigree, I must confess at times I have been at a loss how to dispose of it in my thoughts. I perceive there are many and various conjectures as to the real person who has been the subject of such notice in the public prints. There are certainly doubts and mystery existing in relation to some of Thomas Williams's children. Among many others, I will only mention one; viz. it appears from the baptismal register, lately obtained from the Romish priest at Caughnawaga, which was accompanied by his affidavit, sworn before one of her Majesty's justices of the peace, stating that to be a true list of the names of the births of the children of Thomas Williams (an Iroquois chief), and no such name as Eleazer is to be found among them in the register. The intervals of the births of the children, being nine in number, are regular, excepting *two*."

I understand that the Rev. Dr. Lothrop, of Boston, in his recent lecture delivered in that city, stated that he had procured facts from Canada, showing that the reason why the name of Eleazer was omitted in the baptismal register was that he was born in the woods on a hunting excursion, which frequently occupies many weeks.

Thus, then, from Eleazer's letters to me, we see that he never expressed a shadow of doubt of his direct lineal descent from the Rev. John Williams, first minister of Deerfield, till the month of July, 1849, nor while giving me a genealogical account of his family, to be published as matter of history.

De Joinville, through his former secretary, Aug. Trognon, in an able letter of February 9, 1853, published in the April number of Putnam's Magazine, says, that he met Mr. Williams at Mackinaw in 1841, and had some conversation with him about the French and Indian wars. One great object of his visit to Mackinaw, Green Bay, and the Upper Mississippi was " to retrace the glorious path of the French, who had first opened to civilization those fine countries." While at Boston, he had probably learned that a person resided at Green Bay, of part Indian descent, by the name of Eleazer Williams, who was preaching to the Indians there, had a good many facts in relation to the subject of his inquiry, and, in the journey and voyage thither, it was perfectly natural for him to make inquiries concerning him on his route ; so that nothing can be made out from the subject of these investigations to establish the fact of his seeking him out to communicate to him the story of his being the son of Louis the Sixteenth. Indeed, the Prince, in the letter of Trognon, absolutely disclaims and denies having had any conversation with Eleazer upon that subject. He says, after having given an account of his conference with him in relation to the French wars : " But there ends all which the article contains of truth concerning the relations of the Prince with Mr. Williams. All the rest, all which treats of the revelation which the Prince made to Mr. Williams concerning the pretended personage of Louis the Seventeenth, is, from one end to the other, a work of the imagination, a fable woven wholesale, a speculation upon the public credulity."

There is an anachronism, too, in the narrative of the Magazine, which has not been corrected there, which states that De Liancourt, who travelled in the United States in the year 1795, visited Colonel Ephraim Williams, the founder of Williams College, at Stockbridge, that year ; when the fact is, that Colonel Williams was killed near Lake George, at the bloody morning scout, so called, on the 8th of September, 1755, forty years before.

The following notice of Eleazer Williams, from the Christian Inquirer of New York, of February 12th, 1853, views the subject in the same light that I do, and is so just that I cannot refrain from copying it.

"To the Editors of the Christian Inquirer.

"Many of your readers will undoubtedly have been made aware, through the February number of Putnam's Monthly, that Rev. Eleazer Williams, missionary to the Onondaga Indians, is no less a personage than Louis the Seventeenth of France, son of Louis the Sixteenth and Marie Antoinette, heir of Hugh Capet, St. Louis, Henry the Fourth, and Louis the Fourteenth, of the French monarchy. It is not a little unfortunate for this interesting romance, that the age of the worthy gentleman in question does not better correspond with the date of the Dauphin's birth. The French prince should now be of the age of sixty-eight, while Mr. Williams has been held to be not much over sixty. And though it is quite possible that a healthy man of sixty-eight should appear seven or eight years younger than he really is, it is not so easy that a man of twenty-eight should appear to be but twenty, and still less easy for a youth of eighteen to go for a boy of ten. Now Eleazer Williams has been known in Massachusetts from his boyhood. As a boy, he lived with the Rev. Mr. Ely, on the Connecticut, where some, we presume, remember him. Dr. Willard, of Deerfield, [probably the writer means Dr. Williams, of Deerfield, as I have been acquainted with him much longer than Dr. Willard has,] remembers seeing him in other parts of the State when he was about the age of twenty. He is descended (by repute at least) from Eunice, daughter of the captive Williams, and again, farther down, from another captive family, of Marlborough, and is one quarter Indian, as his physiognomy, it must be confessed, pretty plainly shows. His journal is, indeed, a most remarkable specimen of evidence, and convinces us that it is most unfortunate for this weak gentleman that the Prince de

Joinville made to him the astonishing disclosure. His head is evidently turned, and the limits between fact and dream have become to him quite hazy. Our private opinion is, the little politeness of the young Frenchman gave an exaltation to his fancy which was not favora bleto his observing nor to his reasoning powers. A wonderful history has been spun out of very small materials. It must indeed have struck even Dr. Hawks and Mr. Hanson as a little singular, that a child treated for so long a time as brutally as the Dauphin was, and reduced to idiocy and affected with scrofula, and brought very dear to death, if he did not actually die, should have survived transportation to our backwoods, and turn out a remarkably healthy man, carrying even to his age uncommon freshness and activity, with no traces whatever of those prolonged cruelties except the scars which should prove them. It is certainly a wondrous instance of the benefits of a sea voyage and an out-door life.

" Mr. Williams has been very unfortunate in losing all the documents on which his story is grounded. This loss, however, is made up by accounts, industriously collected by the Rev. Mr. Hanson, of many mysterious journeys of Frenchmen into parts of the country where Mr. Williams was, some of whom kissed him when he was a boy, and others gave him books for his Indians when he was a man. Louis Philippe himself made a journey down the Ohio and Mississippi on his account. We think, however, that, in the present state of France, Mr. Williams had better cut off his posterity and take the royal estates. They would have been of more value than his claim.   M."

The Christian Register of February 26th, 1853, published at Boston, says: " The Rev. Dr. Lothrop of this city delivered a lecture on Monday evening, before the Mercantile Library Association, on the 'lost Dauphin,' in which he examined the claims of the Rev. Eleazer Williams. The speaker had known Mr. Williams for twelve years, visited him in

1845, at his residence in Wisconsin, and received two visits from him in Boston. In his opinion, there is not a particle of evidence in Mr. W.'s favor, except what depends upon his ' say so.' " The Transcript, from which we take this statement, gives the following interesting report on one portion of it : " It appears that Mr. Williams came to Boston with his whole property, consisting of a considerable tract of land in Wisconsin, encumbered by a bond and mortgage to the amount of eighteen hundred dollars, which bond in the course of trade had fallen into the hands of parties in this city who could not grant a renewal of extension. In twenty-four hours from the time these facts became known to Mr. Lothrop, he was enabled, through the kindness of the late Amos Lawrence, to hand to Mr. Williams a check for the whole amount, and to send him home with his bond in his possession, redeemed and cancelled."

The following is an extract from a letter which I have recently received from the late Governor Charles K. Williams, of Vermont. ' It was written about a fortnight before his death. No man was better qualified to judge upon this subject than Governor Williams. He had lived quite near him for a long period, in the early part of his life.

" *Rutland, Vt., February 26th*, 1853.

" Dr. Williams : —

" My dear Sir, — I was much pleased to receive yours of the 18th instant. I had noticed the articles in relation to the Rev. Eleazer Williams, and can only say, that I have never had any doubt that he was of Indian extraction, and a descendant of Eunice Williams. His father and mother were both of them at my father's house, although I cannot ascertain definitively the year. I have known him for a long time, saw him at Plattsburg in the year 1812, and before at my father's. Has been at my house three or four times within the last two years. I have never conversed with him much on the subjec of his being the Dauphin, as he probably understood, from what I did say, that I had no faith at all in his being any thing else than a descendant from Eunice. Although I cannot fix upon any particular *data*, yet my impression is the same as yours, that he was born in 1790.

"Eleazer's mother is said to be alive, but, I believe, does not favor his pretensions. I have the impression that the family of Thomas Williams reside in Caughnawaga, a village near Montreal, and if there is any record of the baptism of the family of Thomas Williams, it will be found there. I hope to see you in the course of the coming spring and summer, and will converse with you freely on the matter. I consider it all as a humbug, and that it will be exploded in the course of a few months.

> "With great respect, I remain
> > "Your friend and humble servant,
> > > "CHARLES K. WILLIAMS."

Such is some of the evidence to show that the Dauphin, if living, cannot be Eleazer Williams.

I shall now endeavor to show, by *direct* and *positive* evidence, that the Dauphin actually *died* at the time pointed out by the most veracious historians.

THE DAUPHIN.

THIERS, in his history of the French Revolution, speaking of the young prince, Louis the Seventeenth, son of Louis the Sixteenth, says, that he died of a tumor of the knee arising from a scrofulous complaint. The royalist agents asserted that he had been poisoned. Alison says: "The 9th Thermidor came too late to save the unfortunate King of France, Louis the Seventeenth. His jailer, Simon, was, indeed, beheaded, and a less cruel tyrant substituted in his place; but the temper of the times would not, at first, admit of any decided measures of indulgence in favor of the heir of the throne. The barbarous treatment he had experienced from Simon had alienated his reason, but not extinguished his feelings of gratitude. On one occasion the inhuman wretch had seized him by the hair, and threatened to dash his head against the wall ; the surgeon, Nautin, interfered to prevent him, and the child next day presented him with two pears, which had been given him for his supper the preceding evening, lamenting, at the same time, that he had no other means of testifying his gratitude. Simon and Heber had put him to the torture, to extract from him an avowal of crimes connected with his mother, which he was too young to understand. After that cruel day, he almost always preserved silence, lest his words should prove fatal to some of his relations. This resolution and the closeness of his confinement soon preyed upon his health. In February, 1795, he was seized with a fever, and visited by three members of the Committee of Public Safety ; they found him seated at a little table, making castles of cards. They addressed to him words of kindness, but could not obtain an answer. In May the state of his health became so alarming, that the celebrated surgeon Desault was directed by the Convention to visit him. His generous attentions assuaged the sufferings of the child's latter days, but could not prolong his life."

Scott, in his Life of Napoleon Buonaparte, thus speaks of the death of the Dauphin : — " The Dauphin we have already described as a promising child of seven years old, at which no offence could have been given, and from which no danger could have been apprehended. Nevertheless, it was resolved to destroy the innocent child, and by means which to ordinary murders seem deeds of charity.

" The unhappy boy was put in charge of the most hardhearted villain whom the community of Paris, well acquainted with where such agents were to be found, were able to select from their band of Jacobins. The wretch, a shoemaker, called Simon, asked his employers ' what was to be done with the young wolf-whelp. Was he to be slain ! ' ' No.' 'Poisoned ? ' ' No.' ' Starved to death ? ' ' No.' ' What then ! ' ' He was to be got rid of.' Accordingly, by a contin-

12

uance of the most severe treatment, — by beating, cold, vigils, fasts, and ill usage of almost every kind, — so frail a blossom was soon blighted. He died on the 8th of June, 1795."

The *Débats*, a French journal devoted to the interest of the Orleans dynasty, in a memoir of the Duchesse d'Angoulême, says that her brother, the Dauphin, expired in his prison on the 8th of June, 1795. (See Littell's Living Age, Vol. XXXI. p. 617.)

The Duchesse d'Angoulême further says, that, at the time he died, three respectable surgeons of France, who saw him at the time of his death, all testified to the fact of his having died at that time.

The Encyclopædia Americana, under the article Louis the Seventeenth, by Eckhard, says unequivocally that Louis the Dauphin died in 1795.

Abbott, in his History of Marie Antoinette, p. 316, speaking of the Dauphin, says : " The patient, inured to suffering, with blighted hopes and a crushed heart, lingered in silence for a few days upon his bed, and died on the 9th of June, 1795, in the tenth year of his age."

Putnam's Magazine for March contains a notice of Beauchesne's Life of Louis the Seventeenth, in two large volumes. He has gathered up all the particulars of the death of the Dauphin from *unquestionable authority*, and he has no possible doubt as to his death at the time alluded to, June 9th, 1795. The following is an extract from his Introduction : —

"I have gone to the source of all facts already known ; I have put myself in relation with all the living persons whom chance or special duty admitted into the Temple during the Revolution ; I have gathered a great deal of information, and have corrected many errors. I have intimately known Lasne and Gomin, the two last keepers of the Tower, and in whose arms Louis the Seventeeth expired. I have not consulted traditions gathered by children from the lips of their fathers, but the recollections of eyewitnesses, religiously preserved in their memories and hearts. I am, then, able to affirm, upon personal investigation, and with certainty, the least circumstance of the events that I recount."

The notice of this book in Putnam's Magazine says : —

"Judging from the internal evidence, this is a perfectly honest book. We have carefully read it through, and are impressed with the spirit of truth and fidelity which appears to breathe in all its pages. Beginning with the birth of the Dauphin, it narrates each event of his life with the affection of a devotee, and the accuracy of a mathematician. The first volume ends with the execution of the father, and the second is almost exclusively occupied with the incidents of his separation from his mother, his subsequent imprisonment, and death. Many of the facts related are new, and all of them are marked with the most tragic and touching interest.

"On the 3d of July, 1793, the Dauphin was committed to the cruel care of Simon, the cobbler, and his wife, who continued in charge of him, either one or the other being constantly in his presence, until the 19th of January, 1794. With regard to this period, M. Beauchesne gives the testimony of those women who were intimate with the wife of Simon, and frequently saw her during her residence at the Temple, as well before as after. Thus they gathered, day by day, from her own lips, the narrative of the brutal treatment of the young prince. Their recollections, added to the facts already notorious, render this chapter the most interesting in the book. After Simon left, the Dauphin was immured in a dungeon, the door of which was nailed up, all light being excluded, and his only communication with the world was through an iron lattice, which was opened from time to time to admit his food.

"In this cell he remained till the 27th of July following, a little more than six months, when the downfall of Robespierre and the advent of the Directory brought a change in his treatment. A man named Laurent, a native of St. Domingo, was appointed by Barras keeper of the children of the ex-king. A humane and well-educated person, although an ardent believer in the revolutionary idea of the time, he was filled with horror on discovering the state of the Dauphin. He brought him out of the pestilential dungeon, washed him, dressed his sores, and caused him to be provided with clothes. When they entered the dungeon, the child, who was not ten years old, was lying in a mass of rags, filth, and vermin, and so reduced and broken, that he did not move, and paid no attention to the many questions that were put to him. Finally, one of the deputies who was present, and who asked him several times why he had not eaten his dinner, which stood untouched on the shelf of the lattice, drew from him the reply, ' No; I want to die.' From this until his reported death, his keepers were comparatively kind, and did all that they dared to render his life tolerable. On the 8th of November, Laurent received a colleague, Gomin, and on the 29th of March, 1795, the former resigned his charge. During this period the boy used often to play draughts with Gomin, and to walk on the terrace of the Tower, until the 25th of January, when his disease made it necessary that he should be removed. He had tumors at all his joints, refused to move, and could hardly be made to speak. Still he understood every thing that was said to him, and on several occasions when alone with Gomin, whom he had learned to love, showed, by gestures and expressions, that he knew who he was, and remembered the father, mother, and sister whom he was never to see more. Once, by his looks and movements, he asked Gomin to take him to his sister's prison, which was in the same building, and when told that it was impossible, said, ' I want to see her once more. O, let me see her again before I die, I pray you!' Gomin took him by the hand, and led him to a chair. The child fell upon his bed in a fainting fit, and when he came to himself, burst into loud weeping.

"When Laurent resigned, he was succeeded by a house-painter named Lasne, who, with Gomin, remained until the end. The new-comer took particular charge of the Dauphin, while Gomin became the jailer of his sister.

"Lasne had often seen the young prince before his imprisonment, and in his conversation with Beauchesne says, 'I recognized him perfectly. His head had not changed; it was still as beautiful as I had seen it in former times; but his complexion was dead and colorless, his shoulders were high, his breast hollow, his legs and arms thin and frail, and large tumors covered his right knee and left wrist.' Lasne treated him with the greatest kindness, and was not absent from him a single day. On the 6th of May, on the demand of his keepers, who represented that his life was in danger, M. Desault, a physician, visited him, and recognized him as the Dauphin. The boy refused to take the medicine ordered till the second day, when Lasne, telling him that he should take it himself, and that he ought to save his friend from such a necessity, the child said, 'You have determined, then, that I should take it; well, give it to me and I will drink it.' On the 31st of May, M. Bellanger, a painter, happened to be the commissary on service for the day, and brought some drawings to show the little invalid. The latter looked at them, finally replied to the questions of the artist, and sat for his own portrait. At the interview with Bellanger, the child gave signs of intelligence by word and look; — and indeed there seems to have been no good reason for supposing that he was ever idiotic; an idea originating in his usual obstinate silence alone. But the very day before he died, he said to Gomin, who told him of the arrest of a commissary who had often been on duty at the Temple, 'I am very sorry, for you see he is more unhappy than we; he deserves his misfortune.' *He died on the 9th of June, at about two o'clock in the afternoon.* On the night previously he said to Gomin, who expressed pity for his sufferings, 'Be consoled; I shall not always suffer.' Some time afterward, Gomin said to him, 'I hope you do not suffer any pain now.' 'O, yes,' was the answer; 'but much less, the music is so beautiful.' As no music was audible, Gomin asked him, ' From what direction do you hear music!' 'From up yonder.' Presently the child exclaimed in ecstasy, ' Among all the voices I hear that of my mother!' Next day, Lasne relieved Gomin from his attendance at the bedside. After a time the child moved, and Lasne asked him how he was; to which he answered, ' Do you think my sister could have heard the music! How much good it would have done her!' Presently he said, ' I have one thing to tell you.' Lasne bent to listen, but the boy was dead.

" The second day after the decease *the corpse was visited, and its identity recognized by above twenty persons, of whom five were officers, and four commissioners on duty at the post.* The *majority* of those persons certified that they had seen the Dauphin at the Tuilleries or the Temple, and knew the dead body to *be his*. The physicians who made the *post mortem* examination certify to a tumor on the inside of the right knee, and another on the left wrist. These tumors had not changed the external skin, but existed under it. After the examination, the body was buried. We give the above account without giving any further opinion on the question than that Mr. Beauchesne is perfectly honest in his conclusions, and that his witnesses will probably be viewed as trustworthy by a great majority of the world."

Beauchesne further says: " Louis of France, the seventeenth of that name, lived only ten years, two months, and two days." His *convictions*, he says, of the Dauphin's death, have " the character of a *certainty authentically demonstrated* "; and he further says, " A curse upon me, if my mind, in possession of the truth, should suffer my pen to lie."

The evidence, then, in relation to the death of the Dauphin, in 1795, is as strong as any which can be found in history in relation to the death of his father, or of Marie Antoinette, his mother, or of almost any other distinguished personage. Equally strong and well-attested testimony must be brought

on the part of the disbelievers of his death, to destroy the
assertions of those historians. These cannot be destroyed by
the testimony of a single individual, or even by numbers, if
they are not equally well attested. They are sufficient to
invalidate the claim of Eleazer Williams to the throne of
France, and to prove that he is not the son of the late Louis
the Sixteenth.

The Paris correspondent of the New York Commercial
Advertiser sends the following paragraph, which has an im-
portant bearing on the romantic claims of the Rev. Eleazer
Williams to be regarded as the veritable son of Louis the
Sixteenth : —

"Mr. Putnam will receive by this steamer a very pithy
and conclusive document from M. de Chaumont, relative to
the use made of his father's name in the famous Bourbon dis-
covery. It is not intended for publication. About twenty
distinct propositions are laid down, in the article on the al-
leged Dauphin, concerning M. de Chaumont, senior, not one
of which is true, or anywhere near true. The errors in dates
are enormous. M. de Chaumont is stated to have arrived
in America in a certain year; he did not arrive there, how-
ever, till eleven years afterward. On his return to France he
is stated to have had an interview with Louis Philippe, in ref-
erence to the Louis the Seventeenth he had seen in the United
States. Now, M. de Chaumont never spoke to Louis Phi-
lippe in the whole course of his life! M. de Chaumont con-
siders his father's name calumniated by the assertion that he
plotted with the Indians against the United States, and that
no contradiction of this calumny would be deemed by him too
formal or too public."

Rev. George E. Day writes, in answer to an inquiry in
respect to his showing Rev. Eleazer Williams a likeness of
Simon the jailer, as stated in Putnam's Magazine, that "the
statement needs some modification to be correct"; that on
seeing the portrait there was no exclamation as alleged ; and,
"upon the whole, I felt then, and have always felt since, that

whatever evidence this recognition might furnish must be derived from the testimony of Mr. Williams himself."

Much more might be written to contradict the articles favoring the Dauphin controversy, but it is not deemed necessary; my object has been rather to prove that Mr. Williams was a descendant of Rev. John Williams, author of " The Redeemed Captive."

THE END.